# THE LONDON LEYLANDS

## THE LAST YEARS OF RTL & RTW OPERATION IN LONDON

# THE LONDON LEYLANDS

## THE LAST YEARS OF RTL & RTW OPERATION IN LONDON

## JIM BLAKE

PEN & SWORD
TRANSPORT

AN IMPRINT OF PEN & SWORD BOOKS LTD.
YORKSHIRE – PHILADELPHIA

FRONT COVER: **One of** the twenty-three RTLs overhauled with roofbox bodies in 1964, RTL73 calls at County Hall on route 170 from Clapton garage in the autumn of 1967.

BACK COVER, TOP: **Relatively few** RTLs and RTWs survive in preservation. One that does is RTL1163, seen at the Barking Bus Rally on 3/4/88. The gentleman standing beside it is the late Frank Tendler, who could quote from memory the entire allocation history of every RTL and RTW bus!

BACK COVER, BOTTOM: **A shortage** of RT training vehicles in the summer of 1978 caused London Transport to hire RT-types from preservationists. These included a few RTLs, the oddest of which was RTL525, which having been exported to Jersey in March 1959 for use by Jersey Motor Transport, had to be re-registered MGP 11P when returned to mainland Britain in 1975. It is seen here leaving Chiswick Works on a training mission on 14/7/78. This RTL was later exported to Spain in 1982.

First published in Great Britain in 2018 by
PEN & SWORD TRANSPORT
An imprint of
Pen & Sword Books Ltd
Yorkshire – Philadelphia

Copyright © Jim Blake

ISBN 978 1 47386 142 8

The right of Jim Blake to be identified as Author of this work has been asserted by him in accordance with the Copyright, Designs and Patents Act 1988.

A CIP catalogue record for this book is available from the British Library

Typeset by Matthew Wharmby

Printed and bound by Replika Press Pvt. Ltd.

Pen & Sword Books Ltd incorporates the Imprints of Aviation, Atlas, Family History, Fiction, Maritime, Military, Discovery, Politics, History, Archaeology, Select, Wharncliffe Local History, Wharncliffe True Crime, Military Classics, Wharncliffe Transport, Leo Cooper, The Praetorian Press, Remember When, Seaforth Publishing and Frontline Publishing.

For a complete list of Pen & Sword titles please contact

PEN & SWORD BOOKS LTD
47 Church Street, Barnsley, South Yorkshire, S70 2AS, England
E-mail: enquiries@pen-and-sword.co.uk
Website: www.pen-and-sword.co.uk

Or
PEN AND SWORD BOOKS
1950 Lawrence Rd, Havertown, PA 19083, USA
E-mail: Uspen-and-sword@casematepublishers.com
Website: www.penandswordbooks.com

# CONTENTS

# ABOUT THE AUTHOR

I was born at the end of 1947, just five days before the 'Big Four' railway companies, and many bus companies – including London Transport – were nationalised by Clement Attlee's Labour government.

Like most young lads born in the early post-war years, I soon developed a passionate interest in railways, the myriad steam engines still running on Britain's railways in those days in particular. However, because my home in Canonbury Avenue, Islington was just a few minutes' walk from North London's last two tram routes, the 33 in Essex Road and the 35 in Holloway Road and Upper Street, my parents often took me on these for outings to the South Bank, particularly to the Festival of Britain which was held there in the last summer they ran, in 1951. Moreover, my father worked at the GPO's West Central District Office in Holborn and often travelled to and from work on the 35 tram. As a result, he knew many of the tram crews, who would let me stand by the driver at the front of the trams as they travelled through the Kingsway Tram Subway. This was an unforgettable experience for a four-year-old! In addition, my home was in the heart of North London's trolleybus system, with route 611 actually passing my home, and one of the busiest and most complicated trolleybus junctions in the world – Holloway, Nag's Head – a short ride away along Holloway Road. Here, the trolleybuses' overhead almost blotted out the sky! Thus from a very early age, I developed an interest in buses and trolleybuses which was equal to my interest in railways, and I have retained both until the present day.

I was educated at my local Highbury County Grammar School, and later at Kingsway College, by coincidence a stone's throw from the old tram subway. I was first bought a camera for my 14th birthday at the end of 1961, which was immediately put to good use photographing the last London trolleybuses in North West London on their very snowy last day a week later. Three years later, I started work as an administrator for the old London County Council at County Hall, by coincidence adjacent to the former Festival of Britain site. I travelled to and from work on bus routes 171 or 172, which had replaced the 33 and 35 trams mentioned above.

By now, my interest in buses and trolleybuses had expanded to include those of other operators, and I travelled throughout England and Wales between 1961 and 1968 in pursuit of them, being able to afford to travel further afield after starting work. I also bought a colour cine-camera in 1965, with which I was able to capture what is now very rare footage of long-lost buses, trolleybuses and steam locomotives. Where the latter are concerned, I was one of the initial purchasers of the unique British Railways 'Pacific' locomotive 71000 *Duke of Gloucester*, which was the last ever passenger express engine built for use in Britain. Other preservationists laughed at our group which had purchased what in effect was a cannibalised hulk from Barry scrapyard at the end of 1973, but they laughed on the other side of their faces when, after extensive and innovative rebuilding, it steamed again in 1986. It has since become one of the best-known and loved preserved British locomotives, often returning to the main lines.

Although I spent thirty-five years in local government administration, with the LCC's successor, the Greater London Council, then Haringey Council and finally literally back on my old doorstep, with Islington Council, I also took a break from office drudgery in 1974/5 and actually worked on the buses as a conductor at London Transport's Clapton Garage, on local routes 22, 38 and 253. Working on the latter, a former tram and trolleybus route, in particular was an unforgettable experience. I was recommended for promotion as an inspector, but rightly thought that taking such a job with the surname Blake was unwise in view of the then-current character of the same name and occupation in the On The Buses TV series and films, and so declined the offer and returned to County Hall!

By this time, I had begun to have my transport photographs published in various books and magazines featuring buses. I had also started off the North London Transport Society, which catered for enthusiasts interested in the subject. In conjunction with this group, I have also compiled and published a number of books since 1977, featuring many of the 100,000 or so transport photographs I have taken over the years.

Also through the North London Transport Society, I became involved in setting up and organising various events for transport enthusiasts in 1980, notably the North Weald Bus Rally which the group took over in 1984; it has raised thousands of pounds for charity ever since. These events are still going strong today.

In addition to my interest in public transport, I also have an interest in the popular music of the late 1950s and early 1960s, in particular that of the eccentric independent record producer, songwriter and manager Joe Meek. In Joe's tiny studio above a shop in Holloway Road (not far from the famous trolleybus junction) he wrote and produced Telstar by The Tornados, which became the first British pop record to make No.1 in America, at the end of 1962, long before The Beatles had even been heard of over there! When Joe died in February 1967, I set up an Appreciation Society for his music, which is still going strong today. His music has a very distinctive sound.

I also enjoy a pint or two (and usually more) of real ale. I have two grown-up daughters, Margaret and Felicity, and three grandchildren, Gracie, Freddie and Oscar, at the time of writing. I still live in North London, having moved to my present home in Palmers Green in 1982.

# INTRODUCTION

L ONDON TRANSPORT'S famous early post-war RT family of buses are, of course, well-known to all transport enthusiasts. More than 7,000 buses of basically similar appearance were delivered, enabling London Transport to reach the peak of standardisation in the early 1950s. Indeed any picture postcard of Central London's landmarks in that period, and in fact for more than a decade or so after that, will show the standard London bus – the RT.

However, although the bodywork of these buses looked similar since all were constructed to resemble London Transport's standard design, many of the buses *were* different.

As will be explained below, the need to build as many new buses as possible after the war forced London Transport to procure them from different manufacturers. The most 'different' of these buses of all were the RTL and RTW classes, which had Leyland chassis adapted to carry bodies similar to, and in many cases interchangeable with, those carried by the majority of the RT family of buses, the AEC Regents built by London Transport's preferred manufacturer. With an immediately noticeable different radiator front, and a much louder engine note, the RTLs and RTWs had a character all of their own, and particularly in the late 1950s and early 1960s they dominated many of the busiest routes serving the City and West End of London. Therefore, any picture postcard from that period will usually feature one of them. By this time, however, many of the RT family of buses had become surplus to requirements due to service cuts, and since the Leyland versions – the RTLs and RTWs – were in a minority, these were some of the first to be withdrawn from service. This process accelerated from the winter of 1962/63 onwards when new Routemasters began to replace them, and once new one-man-operated types also came on the scene in 1968, their fate was sealed and all were withdrawn by the end of that year. It was therefore natural that they became firm favourites with London transport enthusiasts, the more so since very many were exported for further use overseas (most notably to Ceylon, present-day Sri Lanka), and most of the last survivors went to the scrapyard. This means that today far fewer RTLs and RTWs survive in preservation when compared pro-rata to their more numerous sisters, the AEC RTs. Because I had advance warning of which routes were due to lose their RTLs and RTWs, and later on exact details of when each RTL was due to be withdrawn, I made a point first of photographing them on the routes soon to lose them, then secondly, from the beginning of 1967, trying to photograph each individual vehicle, which I succeeded in doing barring a handful of unlucky RTLs withdrawn early owing to accident damage. Some of the results of my efforts are presented in this book, most having never been published before.

As will be seen, I have given brief historical notes for each vehicle illustrated. Vehicle overhaul and allocation transfer dates are taken from my own records compiled at the time. These were derived from news-sheets provided by the PSV Circle, and I wish to record my thanks to them. Details of the RTLs' and RTWs' subsequent fates came largely from John A.S. Hambley's excellent book The RTL and RTW classes after London Transport. Thanks go to him, too, as well as to Colin Clarke and John Scott-Morgan, for helping make this book possible.

*Jim Blake*
Palmers Green
28 May 2015

**This view** in York Road, Waterloo on a very wet 17/5/67, clearly shows the difference in width between the wider RTW class and the RTL class. RTW168 on training duties overtakes Tottenham-based RTL1270 on route 171. Although the latter route kept RTLs until June 1968, this one was withdrawn shortly after this picture was taken. It is also evident how the all-metal Leyland body on the RTW has a thinner waistband than the Park Royal-bodied RTL, though also that both bodies are to the same basic London Transport design.

# LONDON'S LEYLANDS IN RETROSPECT

ALTHOUGH LONDON TRANSPORT, that is both the pre-war and wartime London Passenger Transport Board, and its post-war successors, in the form of the London Transport Executive (1948-62) and London Transport Board (1963-69) were always associated with buses with AEC chassis and engines, the fleet also had a fair number of those with Leyland chassis, engines and running units. This was even despite the fact that, originally, AEC had begun life as part of the 'empire' of London Transport's predecessor, The London General Omnibus Company, and that until the two builders became part of the same owning group, AEC and Leyland were deadly rivals.

Before the war, London Transport had standardised on AEC Regent chassis for its double-deckers, the famous STL class, yet had also purchased a hundred Leyland Titan double- deckers with very similar bodywork and classified them STD. Similarly, although AEC Regals and the side-engined Q types were favoured for single-deck buses and Green Line coaches before the war, a considerable number of Leylands were also acquired, in the form of the C, CR and TF classes. And at this period, almost half of London's trolleybuses were Leylands, too, despite the remainder being AECs!

# POST-WAR VEHICLE SHORTAGES

After the Second World War had ended, London's bus fleet was in a very sorry state. Quite apart from a number of vehicles being lost and damaged through enemy action, many time-expired buses had to be kept on in service long beyond their intended withdrawal dates. In addition, the tram to trolleybus conversion programme had to be halted when the London Blitz began in September 1940, and after the war it was decided to replace the remaining thousand or so trams with motor-buses instead. This merely added to the number of new buses that needed to be built.

London Transport had already designed their famous AEC RT-type double-deckers before the war, with the prototype appearing just before hostilities began, and another 150 'production' RTs being built before wartime requirements for tanks and aeroplanes obliged their building to be suspended. Advances in vehicle technology on the one hand meant a modified RT design appeared after the war, but on the other hand, shortages of manpower and materials meant that production of these new buses did not resume until the spring of 1947. Ideally, London Transport, who were already reaching a high degree of standardisation before the war began, would have liked all their new buses to have been RTs, but with the numbers needed over a fairly short spell of time (seven years as it turned out), it was impossible for AEC to supply enough chassis. By now AEC was a separate company, and in any case all other British bus operators were also desperate for new buses, many of them already being AEC customers too.

# LONDON TRANSPORT TURNS TO LEYLAND

The final solution to London Transport's problem, after a year or so's worth of AEC RTs had been delivered, was to turn to Leyland again. A batch of Leyland Titan PD1s had already been delivered in 1946 and tagged onto the STD class to help make ends meet; thus it was agreed that Leyland would adapt their now-current Titan PD2 chassis to enable it to fit RT-style bodies which, to take London Transport's quest for rigid standardisation even further, could be interchanged upon overhaul with those carried by RTs. This meant, basically, that their chassis mountings had to be altered to accommodate these bodies.

The first RTs had been fitted with bodies actually built at the LPTB's Chiswick Works where, because bodies usually took longer to overhaul than chassis, it was standard practice to interchange them at overhaul and also have a few 'float', or spare, bodies built to ensure that buses were returned to service as quickly as possible.
Even prior to the formation of the nationalised London Transport Executive at the beginning of 1948, bodies were no longer built at Chiswick. Instead, contracts were placed with outside body manufacturers to body the RTs to London Transport's standard design. Initially, Park Royal Vehicles and Weymann's of Addlestone (both within LT's operating area) did so, followed by the Saunders Engineering & Shipyard Company of Beaumaris, Anglesey and Cravens of Sheffield. The latter bodies were considerably non-standard, and could not be interchanged with those built by the other three companies at overhaul.

The first RTL actually had a body that had been intended for an RT (RT657), and was one of the early Park Royal examples carrying a roof route number box. It was to be the only RTL bearing such a body until a couple of others gained them on overhaul in 1956. Moreover, this first RTL was not numbered RTL1, but RTL501! The reason for this was that, by the time it appeared, contracts had also been signed with Leyland Motors for a batch of 500 PD2 Titans with Leyland-built bodywork to London Transport's RT-style design. However, these had 8ft wide chassis (as opposed to the then-standard 7ft 6ins for other London buses), so it was decided to classify them RTW (=RT Wide), and they became RTW1-500, first appearing in 1949.

# RTL BODY TYPES

Meanwhile, RTL1 onwards had begun to appear towards the end of 1948. The first 550 of them (including the prototype) all had Park Royal bodies that could be exchanged at overhaul with RTs, but to confuse matters further, another variation of the type appeared in 1949. To speed up the replacement of worn-out pre-war and wartime buses, and many of the surviving trams, the Metro-Cammell Carriage & Wagon Company of Birmingham were contracted to body 450 of the RTLs, RTL551-1000. Known to staff and enthusiasts alike as the 'MCW' or 'Met-Cam' RTLs, these were at first sight identical to RTs and other RTLs body-wise, but in fact were substantially different. Instead of being of 'composite' construction (i.e. wood and metal), they were of all-metal construction, as were the RTWs. In addition, they had different mountings so they could not be interchanged with other body makes, although they were changed at overhaul within their own batch. There was also a visual difference, in that the cream waistband on them was thinner than that on other body makes. Park Royal-bodied RTLs resumed again at RTL1001, and apart from RTL1307 which had a Weymann body when new, continued to RTL1600. The last thirty-one, RTLs 1601-1631 also had Weymann bodies when new. In any case, Weymann and Park Royal bodies were freely interchanged with those on RT chassis throughout the time the body-change system affected the two classes (1955-65) at London Transport's Aldenham Works, though for some reason no RTL ever gained a Saunders body upon overhaul.

Similarly, it seems odd that the RTL class ended abruptly at RTL1631 late in 1954. With the larger RT class (which reached RT4825) there had been intentions of building more than 5,000 of them. However this was scaled back when it was realised that bus usage was dropping as their production runs ended in 1954, so much so that, indeed, some RTs and RTLs remained in store unused until as late as 1958/59. There have also been tales circulated that there were more RTLs actually built, but not needed and sold 'on the quiet' to countries behind the Iron Curtain when not needed in London. But this is very unlikely and these tales probably arise from the fact that some RTLs which had been used in London service were sold to operators in Yugoslavia in the early 1960s. The most likely explanation for the odd number of RTLs, 1631, is that one of the class, RTL1222, was completely destroyed by fire when quite new, at a time when they were still being built, so perhaps an additional example was ordered to replace it.

# RTL AND RTW ALLOCATION

Operation-wise, all London's 'Leyland RTs', the RTLs and RTWs, were originally built as red buses for Central Area use. At first, the wider RTWs were not permitted to work in Central London's congested streets, but after tests were carried out in 1950 to prove their extra six inches was not a problem, most were reallocated specifically to work busy routes through the City and West End, such as the 6, 8, 11 and 15, where the extra space became an advantage, especially to conductors squeezing between standing passengers! Similarly, many RTLs were at first based at outer London garages, for example Barking, Seven Kings and Sidcup, but at the time of the bus strike and service cuts of 1958, these were exchanged with RTs and, for the most part, also worked routes through the City and West End, though by now, withdrawal of the class owing to the surplus of buses that already existed before the 1958 cuts had already begun. In an attempt to use some of the surplus RTLs, eighteen of them were overhauled in green Country Area livery in 1959 and sent to Hatfield garage for trunk routes 303 and 303A. However, they were not popular with crews owing to their steering being heavier and more sluggish than the RTs, and were soon withdrawn and demoted to driver trainer duties. This, indeed, was the beginning of the end for the RTLs as crews elsewhere also had that opinion of them; moreover they were now in a minority when compared to the more numerous RTs. Some surplus RTLs, though, were overhauled and used to replace trolleybuses at Clapton and Bow garages in the spring and summer of 1959, remaining there until almost the end, as we shall see later in this book.

On the other hand, all of the roomier RTWs remained in service until the autumn of 1963, when some were demoted to training duties following replacement by RMs on route 14. But after that their demise was swift – all had been withdrawn from public service by mid-May 1966, though they survived on training duties until early 1971.

Usually, owing to the need for standardisation with spare parts etc., RTLs and RTWs were not mixed in allocation with RTs, with the notable exception of Upton Park garage which had a large allocation of RTWs for busy route 15, but RTs for all of its other routes. When they were replaced by Routemasters from the end of 1962 onwards, it was often the case that RMs with Leyland engines were used to replace them: in fact they had the same Leyland 0600 engines as the RTLs and RTWs anyway.

# BODY OVERHAULS AND RESULTANT ODDITIES

After London Transport had decided to withdraw the RTWs and RTLs en masse before the majority of RTs were withdrawn, overhauling of them at Aldenham Works ceased. The last RTWs were overhauled early in 1962, followed by the last 'Metro-Cammell'-bodied RTLs in the autumn of 1963. A 'hiccup' occurred in the output of the latter, in that one vehicle, RTL626, which should have been within their number-range (RTL550-1000) and therefore sent out with an MCCW body, which as stated above could only be fitted to RTLs within that range since these bodies were not interchangeable with standard Park Royal or Weymann ones, appeared from Aldenham in January 1962 carrying a Park Royal body. Thus when the 'Metro-Cammell' bodies' overhaul cycle came to an end the following year, one of those bodies was left over! It appeared on RTL1005, which should not have been able to carry such a body, but which presumably was the stock-number closest to their batch being overhauled at the time! Standard RTLs (i.e. those with Park Royal or Weymann bodies) continued to be overhauled until January 1965. In their final year, many were given older bodies hitherto on RT chassis, with newer RTL bodies being fitted to RTs which were expected to last longer, as indeed they did. This resulted in twenty-three RTLs appearing with roof route-box bodies, a combination that had not been seen in service since 1958, when in any case only three had ever been in use. This was not quite the end, since delays in production of new buses meant that an additional one hundred RTLs were overhauled, with body-changes, at Aldenham between July 1965 and January 1966. These could immediately be identified by their having the then-new livery with a grey waistband, instead of the previous cream one. Sadly, these would not last long in service.

# WITHDRAWAL AND DISPOSAL – THE FINAL YEARS

The usual criteria for withdrawal was the expiry of the buses' certificates of fitness, which usually lasted for seven years after their last Aldenham overhaul. At first, as RTLs were replaced both by new Routemasters and by RTs displaced from elsewhere, those whose certificates of fitness expired first were withdrawn first, with any that were overhauled more recently moved on to replace other RTLs elsewhere. However, after the holocaust of 'Black Saturday', 7 September 1968, when upon the first stage of London Transport's 'Reshaping Plan' all two hundred or so RTLs based in their former East End strongholds of Bow, Hackney, Poplar and West Ham garages perished in one stroke, even those overhauled less than three years earlier were withdrawn, leaving some that had been done a year or more earlier to soldier on until the end. This came for the whole class, at Willesden garage, at the end of November. After the last RTLs were withdrawn from public service, a number that had been commandeered for Aldenham or Chiswick Works staff buses in 1960/61 soldiered on for a few more months. General replacement of these by RTs began in the latter part of 1969, and the last one ran in May 1971.

Once general withdrawal of RTLs began at the end of 1962, when they were directly replaced by new RMs on routes 37 and 73, they were at first replaced on a route-by-route basis, as also were the RTWs. However, from the summer of 1965 they were instead replaced on a garage-by-garage, gradual basis, mostly by RTs displaced from elsewhere. This process was accelerated by former Country Area RTs that had been replaced either by new Country Area RMLs, or by their routes converting to single-deck one-man operation, being overhauled or in some cases merely repainted in red and drafted in to the Central Area to replace them. The last RTWs were withdrawn from service in May 1966, after which the remaining RTLs followed suit. During their last two years, 1967 and 1968, only two RTL-operated routes were replaced by RMs. One was Hackney garage's share of route 22 in the autumn of 1967, the other was route 60 on 7 September 1968. Although the 60 was withdrawn, in effect it was replaced by new RM-operated route 8B which operated the same routeing between Oxford Circus and Cricklewood. All other RTL routes were allocated RTs displaced from elsewhere.

A few RTLs and RTWs remained in London Transport stock, as staff buses and driver trainers respectively, into the 1970s, by which time the Greater London Council had assumed control of the organisation. However, they did not last long. The last trainer RTWs were retired in January 1971, followed by the last staff bus RTL in May that year.

# AFTER LIFE

As mentioned earlier, very many RTLs and RTWs were exported to Ceylon for further use, including more than half of the 500-strong RTW fleet. A good few RTLs also saw further use in South Africa and, somewhat oddly, Yugoslavia. In Britain, a small number of RTWs and a few dozen RTLs also found use with independent bus operators (notably Barton of Chilwell, who acquired some as late as 1967/68) as well as being used as staff or school buses. After the final withdrawal of the RTLs in 1968, however, most went for scrap, as did the vast majority of the RTLs and RTWs that had been retained as staff buses or driver trainers. Only a small number of each type survive in preservation.

**Typifying how** London's RTLs looked in the early 1960s, RTL536 stands at the Euston Square terminus of route 77 on 5 May 1962. It has just been overhauled at Aldenham and, as may be seen, still carries an offside route number stencil behind the lower deck windows. These were discontinued some eighteen months later. Interestingly, the Weymann body this RTL carries, No.9224, was new to RTL1629 late in 1954, and this vehicle was stored out of use until 1958. Its May 1962 overhaul was the only one it ever had, since it was withdrawn five years later; thus body No.9224 only saw some nine years' service in London! The bus is based at Stockwell garage, which was opened in 1951 to house tram replacement routes, and had a very large allocation of RTLs. Although Stockwell's allocation on route 77 ceased in 1963, the garage still ran RTLs on its subsidiaries 77A and 77C until they were replaced by RTs in the summer of 1967. RTL536 ended its career with London Transport at Clapton garage earlier in the that year, eventually being sold to Ceylon in May 1968.

**Seen in** Gower Street by the northern entrance to Euston Square Station, Chalk Farm's RTL780 is seen on the busy route 24 on 9 November 1963, at a time when new RMs were gradually replacing RTWs on this route. This is one of the 450 RTLs with all-metal MCCW bodies, and when compared to that in the previous picture, its narrower waistband is of note. It still has its offside route stencil place; by now these were being removed. Though last overhauled only in June 1962, this RTL moved to Walworth after the 24's RM conversion, and had been withdrawn by the end of 1965. It was sold to Ceylon in January 1966. This was a fate common to many RTLs, and over half the RTW class.

**On a** grey and cold Saturday, 28/12/63, Middle Row's RTL561, another MCCW example, calls at Paddington station on route 7, which by now is receiving new RMs, too. Note how both this RTL and the RM in front of it, which is on the 36 group of routes, are no longer showing offside route numbers. This RTL remained at Middle Row until replaced by RTs on routes 28 and 187A in the latter part of 1965, eventually going to Ceylon at the end of 1966.

**I hope** readers will forgive me for including this picture with the railings partially obstructing the view of Clapton's RTL285! It was taken at Manor House Station on Saturday, 8 February 1964, the first day of operation of new route 253A, which was to be the last new route introduced using RTLs. Somewhat curiously, it followed the very busy trolleybus replacement route 253 (which used RMs) from Finsbury Park station to Cambridge Heath station, from where it then followed the 170 via Shoreditch and Old Street to Bloomsbury. Quite how crews coped on the smaller, slower RTLs on the very busy section through Stamford Hill is a mystery to me, having myself conducted RMs on the 253 during 1974/75! This view nicely shows the driver's white uniform hat, something long discontinued by the time I was on the buses, along with the notice in the rearmost lower deck window proclaiming the new route's introduction. The 253A was withdrawn at the end of March 1968, whereas RTL285 was overhauled again in December 1964, working at first at Hackney garage, then Victoria (Gillingham Street) and Wandsworth. It finally moved to Poplar late in 1966, where it remained until withdrawn on 'Black Saturday', 7 September 1968. It went for scrap in May 1969.

**Busy route** 41, running between Tottenham Hale and Highgate, Archway Station, had been the first to operate the wider RTWs, in the autumn of 1949. By now, when Tottenham's RTW163 was seen at the St. John's Tavern, Archway terminus of the 41 on 10 February 1964, they were being replaced by new RMs on this route. This one was one of several moved south to replace RTs at Brixton garage on routes 95 and 109, but it too had been withdrawn by the end of 1965 and was sold to Ceylon in January 1966. Behind it is an RF which has worked short to Archway on the 210, the first route to be operated by red RFs back in September 1952.

**At this** period, most RTWs ran on busy routes working through the City and West End, of which the 15 was a prime example. In the evening rush hour of 28 February 1964, RTW385 loads up at Aldwych. Its blind display indicates that it is running in the Upton Park garage, rather than continuing to the 15's usual eastern terminus at East Ham, White Horse. This one saw further service at Brixton garage and was finally exported to Ceylon in August 1967.

**Many of** the London bus routes local to my home in Canonbury were operated by RTLs in the early 1960s. One was the busy 30, running from Hackney Wick to Roehampton and operated by Putney (Chelverton Road) and Hackney garages. Here on 9/3/64, RTL1537 from the latter garage calls at St. Mary's parish church, Upper Street, on its way south. Route 30 converted to RM operation in the summer of 1964, resulting in this RTLs withdrawal. However, because it had a newer Park Royal body dating from late 1954 (No.9080, originally new to RTL1510), this body was switched with an earlier unoverhauled one from an RT before the RTL was sold at the end of 1965, and put into the Aldenham overhaul system for out-shopping on an RT, thus seeing several years' further service. The vehicle was one of several RTLs sold to Barton of Chilwell, Nottinghamshire and saw almost five years further with them.

**Another RTL**-operated route local to me was the 171, which had replaced Kingsway Subway tram route 33 in April 1952. Here also on 9/3/64, Tottenham RTL1558 calls at Essex Road station on its long journey to Forest Hill. This RTL also carried a newer body (No.9122, new to RTL1552) but, having been overhauled with that one in April 1962, was overhauled again in December 1965 (as one of the extra 100 RTLs dealt with later that year) releasing the newer body for output on an RT. By chance, it returned to Tottenham where it stayed until RTs replaced RTLs on the 171 in June 1968. After that, it moved to West Ham where it finally perished on 'Black Saturday', 7 September 1968. In doing so, it was one of the last RTLs to change allocation when still in service. It finally went for scrap at the end of 1969.

On the same occasion, Upton Park RTW105 lays over in Aldgate bus station, as many 'spreadover' buses did on route 15 at the time, working 'shorts' from there to its western terminus at Ladbroke Grove. Another RTW stands behind it, as does an RTL on route 25. However, new RMs had begun to enter service replacing RTWs on the 15, and within a month, all would be gone from Upton Park. This particular one was demoted to driver training duties, on which it survived until June 1970. It went for scrap in April 1971.

**Surplus RTLs** were also used to replace trolleybuses at Clapton and Bow depots in the spring and summer of 1959. In the latter case, new bus route 26 running from Aldgate to Leyton via Whipps Cross replaced trolleybus route 661, and here at Aldgate on 6/4/64, Bow RTL1456 has just arrived on this route. Note the RTLs missing radiator badge and the trolleybus traction standard still in place behind it. Two months after this picture was taken, RTL1456 was overhauled again, gaining a roofbox body. It saw service in that form at Tottenham garage until withdrawal four years later and finally went for scrap in May 1969. Meanwhile, route 26 was withdrawn at the end of 1966.

**Route 14** had been jointly worked by Holloway RTs and Putney (Chelverton Road) RTWs prior to its conversion to RM operation in the autumn of 1963, but a year later, on 8/10/64, this view finds Putney's RTL1030 working it in heavy traffic in Euston Road. RTLs were allocated there for routes 85, 85A and 93 at this time, but replaced by RTs a year later. This RTL saw further use at Middle Row, Walworth, Cricklewood and Stockwell garages prior to withdrawal in the spring of 1967 and sale to Ceylon at the end of that year.

**My local** 172 was also a tram replacement route, having replaced Kingsway Subway tram route 35 in April 1952. An oddity in the early 1960s was that it ran beyond its usual West Norwood, Thurlow Arms terminus to Norwood garage on Sundays, which is what Camberwell RTL1193 is doing here when seen outside St. Mary's Church, Upper Street, Islington on 18/10/64. The following week, route 172 was withdrawn on Sundays and replaced by new Sunday-only route 188A, thus this working never happened again. When Camberwell lost its RTLs in the summer of 1966, this one was transferred to Clapton, where it served for another year before withdrawal. It too ended up in Ceylon, being one of the last RTLs to be exported there in July 1968.

**By 22/10/64**, replacement of RTs and RTLs on route 137 was well underway, but RTL1105 from Victoria (Gillingham Street) garage is still working it when seen just after passing beneath the North London Line railway bridge in Camden Gardens on its way to Highgate, Archway Station. This RTL moved to Camberwell garage after the conversion, moving on to Clapton in the summer of 1966 and being withdrawn early in 1967. It was sold in April of that year and exported to Canada, where it became a sightseeing bus on Prince Edward Island.

**Just around** the corner, the other side of the track, from the previous picture, Chalk Farm MCCW-bodied RTL600 stands at the Camden Gardens terminus of route 3. This was next in line for RM conversion, which was completed by the end of the year. RTL600 also moved to Camberwell for a few months, being withdrawn in the summer of 1965 and sold to Cape Town Tramways in October that year.

**A quiet** Sunday, 17 January 1965 sees Walworth RTW285 apparently abandoned in High Holborn whilst working route 45. The reason must be that the driver has had to pay a visit to the subterranean 'Gents' in the middle of the road. Perhaps this is not surprising in view of the 45's long and meandering route at this period from South Kensington to Hampstead Heath via Battersea, Clapham Junction, Clapham Common, Stockwell, Brixton, Camberwell, Elephant & Castle, Blackfriars, Holborn and Kings Cross! Shared with Chalk Farm garage, the 45 lost its RTWs in the winter of 1965, when this one was withdrawn. It was sold to Ceylon in June 1966.

**On this** very gloomy Sunday, Willesden RTW98 heads for home along Cheapside with an RTL on route 25 in pursuit. It incorrectly shows a front via blind for the route's rush hour journeys between Kilburn Park Station and Wembley Trading Estate. Conversion of route 8 to RM operation began three days later, and this RTW moved on to Brixton prior to withdrawal. It too was eventually sold to Ceylon, at the end of 1966. Note the newspaper placard on the right, which tells of Sir Winston Churchill's final illness. He died a week after this picture was taken.

Six RTW-operated routes converged at Bank at this period, but by now their days were numbered. These were the 6, 6A, 8, 11, 22 and 76 – a seventh, the 15, having lost them in April 1964. Here, Riverside's RTW140 is seen on one of their strongholds, route 11, which would retain them until the end of January 1966. This one did not last that long, being sold to Ceylon in November 1965 after withdrawal in the summer.

Route changes at the end of January 1965 saw route 176 withdrawn north of Waterloo on Saturdays. On 13/2/65, Walworth RTW408 arrives there, but has managed to knock down and run over an unattended bicycle propped up at the kerbside, and this has become wedged beneath it! In this view, a police officer arrives to inspect the damage. RTWs lasted at Walworth on this route until the end of 1965, but this one had been withdrawn before the end, being sold in December, once again to Ceylon.

**Seen at** Waterloo's Cornwall Road bus terminus the same day, Hackney RTW176 is about to work weekday route 6A's Saturday afternoon extension beyond Hackney Wick to Leyton Town Hall, which involved crossing the River Lea alongside single-deck route 236. Conversion of the 6 group of routes to RM was imminent at this time, and this RTW was withdrawn as a result of it. It was sold in September, unusually to the London coach and school contract operator Isadore Margo of Penge, with whom it stayed for two years or so before conversion to a racing car transporter! Although route 6A was to be withdrawn upon Reshaping on 'Black Saturday', 7 September 1968, new route 26 appeared in July 1992 following its route from Waterloo to Hackney Wick (though without the Leyton extension) and still exists today.

**On Saturdays** at this period, journeys on route 6 from the west terminated at Aldwych, where Willesden RTW20 stands beside St. Mary-le-Strand church also on 13/2/65. This was one of the last RTWs to be overhauled, in March 1962, and remained at Willesden until their last route, the 176, lost them and was eventually sold to Ceylon at the end of 1966. Today, all buses on route 6 terminate at Aldwych, the route's eastern section having been taken over by new route 26 in July 1992.

**Although Tottenham's** RTWs on route 41 had been replaced by RMs in February 1964, others remained at the garage for routes 76 and 106. On the former, RTW266 waits at the traffic lights by Westminster Station on 26/2/65. New RMLs replaced RTWs on this route in the autumn of 1965 as part of comparative trials with XA class Leyland Atlanteans which worked route 24, with the types being swapped in the spring of 1966. By then this RTW had been withdrawn, and it was sold to Ceylon in June that year.

**A peculiar** route to operate at this period was the Saturday-only 6B, which ran from Kensal Rise to Hackney, as did the daily route 6, but then continued via former trolleybus route 257 to Chingford. It was shared between RMs worked by Walthamstow garage and RTWs from Willesden, whose RTW274 has worked short to Aldwych on 6/3/65. The following week, new RMs began to replace RTWs at Willesden on the 6 and 6B. This one moved on to Brixton for a few months, but was sold in January 1966. It was yet another RTW to end up in Ceylon!

**On 29/3/65**, Hackney RTW186 is one of two crossing from Aldwych into The Strand on route 6 bound for Kensal Rise. Two days later, new RMs arrived at Hackney to replace them. It was withdrawn as a result, and sold to Cape Town Tramways, South Africa in June.

**Route 74** was a stronghold of RTW operation for many years, linking Camden Town with Putney and Roehampton. On 15/5/65, Riverside RTW400 gleams in the sun as it loads up at Hyde Park Corner on a Saturday short working to Earls Court. RMs replaced these RTWs in the autumn of 1965. It then moved south to Brixton, remaining there until the spring of 1966. After more than two years gathering dust in store at Poplar garage where it had been prepared for sale to Ceylon, it was instead sold to one of the Yorkshire dealers, but instead of being scrapped it saw a few months' further use with small independent fleets before ending up in a Barnsley scrapyard in May 1970.

**On the** same day, Battersea RTW264 stands in the yard of Victoria, Gillingham Street garage, where route 39 terminated on Saturdays. During the week, this route continued to Finsbury Park station with a further extension to Tottenham garage in rush hours. Shared with Chalk Farm garage, the 39 also lost its RTWs towards the end of 1965. This one was withdrawn as a result, and sold to Ceylon in June 1966.

**The last** route from Willesden garage to use RTWs was the 46. They are imminently due for replacement by some of the last new RMs as RTW427 arrives at Waterloo on 20/5/65. It moved on to Chalk Farm until withdrawal towards the end of the year and was sold to Ceylon in December 1966.

**Somewhat oddly**, Peckham, Rye Lane garage had its RTs replaced by RTLs that had been displaced by new RMs early in 1963 in order to speed up the withdrawal of early 3RT3s, as had also happened at Brixton on route 133. By now, though, these RTLs were due to be replaced by RTs again in the autumn of 1965. Here, on 21/5/65, MCCW-bodied RTL602 loads up in Addington Street, Waterloo, with County Hall, my place of employment at the time, as a backdrop. Many of the RTs that replaced Rye Lane's RTLs had become available from the Country Area, where they had been replaced by new RMLs. This RTL moved on to nearby Camberwell and Walworth garages, and after replacement by RTs at the latter towards the end of 1966, was used as a staff bus to cover the repainting of the permanent RTL staff bus fleet during 1967. It then languished in store for nearly two years until finally going for scrap in June 1969 when it was one of the last Metro-Cammell-bodied RTLs in London Transport stock.

**On the** same day, Stockwell RTL1619 is seen heading south along Marsham Street, behind Westminster Abbey, on route 88. In common with many RTLs in this batch, it did not enter service until 1958, and when overhauled in 1962 gained a Weymann body that had been new to its batch, No.9201, originally on RTL1606. It was overhauled again in September 1965, gaining an earlier body, with No.9201 being fitted to an RT. It went to Clapton garage, remaining here until ousted by RTs in late 1967 and then moving to Bow, where it perished on 'Black Saturday', 7 September 1968. It finally went for scrap in February 1970 after gathering dust in Poplar garage for more than a year.

At this period, Willesden garage had a Saturday allocation on route 18. On 22/5/65, their RTW481 arrives at Paddington Green on a short working shortly before the last RTWs were withdrawn from Willesden upon the RM conversion of route 46. It never ran again in London after that, eventually being sold to Ceylon in June 1966. Curiously, despite the 18's main allocation being RM-operated, RMs did not work the 18 from Willesden; RTLs allocated there for the 52, 176 and 226 did so instead.

The long 68 route, running from Chalk Farm to South Croydon, was operated by RTs from Norwood and South Croydon garages at this time, but by RTLs from Chalk Farm. Here, on 29/5/65, their RTL123 passes the Old Vic theatre in Waterloo Road. This had last been overhauled in August 1960 and was due for early withdrawal, which came when RTs replaced Chalk Farm's RTs in the autumn of 1965. Eventually, it was sold to Ceylon in January 1967.

**On the** same day, Walworth RTL1473 has worked a 184 Saturday journey to Westminster, Horse Guards Avenue rather than traversing the whole Embankment loop as this tram replacement route did in both directions during the week. This too is due for early withdrawal, and was sold to Ceylon in December 1965.

**A smart**-looking Riverside RTL1447 is seen in Park Lane on route 74 on Whit Monday, 7/6/65. This is in fact an odd working, since RTWs were still allocated to the 74 at the time. RTLs based at Riverside for routes 27, 88 and 91 were replaced by RTs shortly after this picture was taken, and this one moved briefly to Highgate and then on to Willesden garage where it remained until the very end of RTL operation at the end of November 1968. After that it was robbed of mechanical parts for its fellows in Ceylon, and the hulk dumped at the rear of Stonebridge Park garage, from where it went for scrap in June 1969.

**The RTWs** based at Brixton garage for the 95 and 109 routes also worked Sunday-only route 57A. Here, also on Whit Monday, 7/6/65, RTW324 loads up in Vauxhall Bridge Road, Victoria for its long run to South Croydon. This one did not survive until the end of RTW operation there in May 1966, being sold to Ceylon that March.

**At this** period, Willesden's last RTWs were being replaced by RMs on route 46, but on 15/6/65, Metro-Cammell RTL734 puts an unusual appearance in on the route and is seen leaving Waterloo for Alperton as another RTL on route 60 follows. Withdrawn when route 52 converted to RM in the autumn of 1966, RTL734 then spent more than two years languishing in the yard of Stonebridge Park garage, where it too was robbed of spare parts for the Ceylon fleet before going for scrap in May 1969.

**Another oddity** seen on 15/6/65 is Chalk Farm RTL383, seen waiting at the traffic lights at Parliament Square on route 24. It substitutes for an RM. Five months later, Leylands of a different type would work route 24 – the experimental XA class Atlanteans. Following replacement on route 68 by RTs later in 1965, this RTL moved first to Hackney garage, then to West Ham where it perished in the holocaust of 'Black Saturday', 7 September 1968. Selected and prepared for export to Ceylon and moved to Grays garage in order to be close to Tilbury Docks from where many were exported, in the event it went for scrap in November 1969.

On 19/6/65, Battersea RTW317 is seen in Buckingham Palace Road working route 39. When Battersea lost their RTWs on this route, which along with their share of the 22 and 31 initially converted to RTL a few weeks later, this RTW moved on to their final London home – Brixton garage. It was sold to Ceylon in December 1966. The 'No Parking' sign on the right is there owing to the influx of coaches to Victoria Coach Station on this summer Saturday.

On the same occasion, Dalston RTW296 heads a line-up of four RTWs in Buckingham Palace Road working a 'short' on route 11 to Aldwych. They may not all necessarily be on the No.11, however, since routes 39 and 46 were also RTW-worked, but not for much longer! This one was yet another to be sold, in June 1966, to Ceylon where it eventually became a single-decker bus and was then converted to a lorry!

By now, a number of RTLs had found their way to small independent fleets in various parts of the country, some of which were in the London Transport operating area. One of these was Roydonian Coaches of Roydon, near Harlow, with whom former RTL1265 is seen in Horse Guards Avenue also on 19/6/65, probably having brought a party to the nearby Whitehall Theatre. This was one of the eighteen RTLs that had been overhauled in green Country Area livery in 1959. It had been sold to Roydonian in September 1963, and saw some six years use with them before being scrapped in late 1970.

**RTWs were** still in charge of route 76 in the summer of 1965, but on 9/7/65, Tottenham RTL201 has found its way onto the route and gleams in the sun as it is caught in the evening rush hour traffic at Westminster Station. Withdrawn late in 1967, it was one of the last RTLs to make the long journey to Ceylon, in July 1968.

**Two RTLs** seen far from home are Highgate garage's RTL849 and RTL1045, which have taken a staff outing on 1/8/65 to Herne Bay, where they are seen in a car park near the seafront. This former trolleybus depot had gained them with a small share of route 196 (transferred from Chalk Farm) two years previously, but a few weeks after this picture was taken, they were replaced by RTs. Metro-Cammell RTL849 saw another year's service at Willesden garage, and was sold to Ceylon in August 1967; standard RTL1045 also went on to work at Willesden and ended up in Ceylon too, though not until April 1968.

**Another Metro-**Cammell-bodied RTL, Clapton's RTL953, waits to turn left from Westminster Bridge onto Victoria Embankment on tram replacement route 170 in the evening rush hour of 9 August 1965. The building seen across the bridge behind the RTL is County Hall, my place of employment at the time. Originally introduced to replace Kingsway Subway tram route 31 in October 1950, the 170 was extended in April 1959 to also replace trolleybus route 555 between Bloomsbury and Leyton. Withdrawn in the autumn of 1966, this RTL was one of relatively few of its type not to go to Ceylon when it was sold for scrap in January 1967.

**Waiting at** the same junction to turn from the Embankment onto Westminster Bridge on 16/9/65 is RTW152, one of the large contingent based at Brixton garage for routes 95 and, as here, 109. This RTW was withdrawn shortly after this picture was taken, but not sold to Ceylon until December 1966. Behind the RTW is one of Grey Green's Harrington 'Cavalier'-bodied coaches, and behind that the original New Scotland Yard headquarters of the Metropolitan Police.

**The furthest** west RTLs reached in the autumn of 1965 was Southall, on Shepherd's Bush's small allocation on route 105. Here, on 21/9/65, their Metro-Cammell RTL876 is seen in Southall's busy South Street immediately before replacement by RTs and withdrawal. It was sold the following month to a dealer, passing to Eynon of Trimsaran in South Wales who operated it for almost two years. Note the lady who has just alighted from the RTL, who typifies the many Asian people already living in Southall fifty years ago.

**Although route** 6A had received new RMs some months previously, Hackney RTW142 has found its way back on to the route when seen at Waterloo bus park on 24/9/65. The garage still had RTWs for routes 22 and 106 until the turn of the year. This one was withdrawn before then, however, being sold to Ceylon in January 1966.

**Until their** replacement by RMs on route 11 at the beginning of February 1966, Riverside RTWs could be seen in place of the usual RTLs on their share of route 27 on Saturdays. On 28/9/65, their RTW429 calls at Camden Town on its long journey from Archway to Teddington. After withdrawal, this RTW was sold to O.K. Motor Services of Bishop Auckland in April 1966, remaining in service with them until late 1972. It was then preserved in their livery, but alas did not last, being scrapped in 1974.

**Just around** the corner, on the Bayham Street stand of route 31 the same day is RTW29, based at Battersea. RTWs from this garage and Chalk Farm shared the route, and were replaced by RTLs later in the autumn of 1965. After withdrawal, this RTW, which had been one of the last to be overhauled (in March 1962) became a driver trainer in the Country Area, initially allocated to Garston garage. It later moved to Amersham, where it remained until August 1969. Despite being stored at Stonebridge Park garage, where many RTLs and RTWs were cannibalised for spares for the Ceylon fleet before going for scrap, once its services were no longer needed, and being sold to a Yorkshire scrap dealer at the end of 1969, it was rescued for preservation in January 1970 and is still going strong more than 45 years later!

**Shortly before** RMs replaced them on Monday to Friday only route 74B, Riverside RTW402 calls at Hyde Park Corner on 1/10/65. This RTW saw further use at Brixton before being sold to Ceylon in June 1966.

**On 5/10/65**, Tottenham RTW209 calls at County Hall, my place of employment at the time, in the evening rush hour bound for Victoria. An RTL on route 172 follows. This RTW was withdrawn a month later when replaced by new RMLs on route 76, and sold in January 1966, also to Ceylon. Note the incorrect use of a canopy number blind in the front number blind box, and that it shows 123, the only trolleybus replacement route ever to have an RTW allocation, which worked from Tottenham until replaced by RMs early in 1964.

**Not far** behind on the same occasion, RTL289 stands in for an RTW on the 76. This was one of Tottenham's small allocation for the 171 and was initially withdrawn in November 1967, upon the start of replacement by RTs at that garage. However a shortage of RTs caused by an increase in their overhauls early in 1968 meant that RTLs like this one that had been moved to storage in Edmonton garage were reinstated. They were finally withdrawn when Tottenham garage received a full RT allocation for the 171 in June 1968. This one languished in store at Bexleyheath until being sold for scrap in May 1969.

**On 7/10/65**, Shepherd's Bush RTL1306 is seen at Parliament Square on route 12, with an RTW on the 76 in pursuit. RTLs at this garage were now rapidly being ousted by RTs, and this one moved to Battersea garage shortly after this picture was taken. It moved on to Willesden for a few months after Battersea too received RTs in the spring of 1967, but was withdrawn and exported to the United States in September of that year.

**Also at** Parliament Square, on 25/10/65, Riverside RTW348 typifies the type of bus that had served busy route 11 for some fifteen years until all were replaced by RMs at the beginning of February 1966. This was another to see out its days at Brixton and, once again, was exported to Ceylon, in January 1967.

**At the** very end of October 1965, some of Tottenham's RTWs on route 76 had already been withdrawn in anticipation of RML conversion, thus the appearance of roofbox RTL143 on the route at lunchtime outside County Hall on 28/10/65 was not entirely unexpected. As mentioned earlier, the first RTL (RTL501) had a roofbox body. These bodies were termed RT10, being modified from the earliest 3RT3 bodies so as to fit both RT and RTL chassis upon overhaul. Two others (RTL9 and RTL36) received them on overhaul in 1956 but were sold in 1958, whilst a third, RTL3, also received an RT10 body but with its entrance and staircase reversed as a pilot for possible sales of RTLs where the rule of the road was left-hand drive. Although this vehicle never operated in this condition, others were so converted after being sold to Yugoslavia. Only in 1964 were twenty-three RTLs overhauled with RT10 bodies originally on RTs, and RTL143 was one of them. Transferred to Dalston garage late in 1967, it was withdrawn when their RTLs were replaced by RTs in June 1968 and sold for scrap in May 1969.

**By 3/11/65** when Chalk Farm RTL684 was seen in Parliament Street on route 39, Metro-Cammell-bodied RTLs such as this were suffering mass withdrawals along with the fast-disappearing RTWs. This one moved on to Wandsworth garage when Chalk Farm's RTLs were replaced by RTs during the winter of 1965/66, and for some reason remained in store there for nearly two years after its withdrawal late in 1966, eventually ending up at the Stonebridge Park dump and going for scrap in May 1969.

**Also in** Parliament Street that day, about to cross into Parliament Square, RTL782 is another Metro-Cammell vehicle, working route 159 from Camberwell garage. This one was withdrawn when Camberwell's RTLs were replaced by RTs in the summer of 1966, and sold to Ceylon in January 1967. When I took this photograph, I had no idea that route 159 would be the last all-day London route with conductor operation forty years later.

**RTL662 seen** on the same day in the familiar setting of County Hall is also a Metro-Cammell-bodied RTL based at Camberwell, working tram replacement route 172. This one came to grief in an accident towards the end of the RTLs' reign at Camberwell in the summer of 1966, and it was cannibalised at Aldenham Works before going for scrap in the August of that year.

**With cardboard** placed in its radiator grille to keep out the cold, RTL596 leaves Waterloo for Colindale when working route 60 from Cricklewood garage on 24/11/65. One of the last Metro-Cammell-bodied RTL's to be overhauled, in October 1963, it was withdrawn early in 1967, and sold to a dealer in May that year, it operated for various Essex independent fleets until being scrapped late in 1972.

**By December** 1965, it was apparent that Brixton garage would be the last stronghold of RTW operation. On a gloomy 3/12/65, their RTW129 loads up at Elephant & Castle on route 95, a tram replacement route that no longer exists today. This RTW had last been overhauled in January 1961, and by now had survived most others overhauled that long ago. It was sold to Ceylon in December 1966.

**Dalston's RTWs** from route 11 had a weekend allocation on route 47 (which was RTL operated during the week alongside Bromley and Catford RT's), thus taking them to the far south of London, as seen by RTW375 standing at a wintry Shoreditch Church terminus on 4/12/65. When the 11 converted to RM two months later, this RTW was withdrawn and it spent some eighteen months in store before sale to Ceylon in August 1967.

**A few** RTWs lingered on at Walworth garage on route 176 until their replacement by RTLs ousted by RTs elsewhere was complete at the end of 1965. Here, RTW499, numerically the penultimate member of the class, loads up in Waterloo Road on 6/12/65. Walworth's other RTW route, the 45, also had RTLs briefly but these were replaced by RMs on 1 January 1966. This RTW spent a year in store before sale to Ceylon in January 1967.

**I hope** readers will forgive my using this rather gloomy shot, which shows roofbox RTL1427 working route 106 from Clapton garage at Stoke Newington station on 16/12/65. The route was shared with Hackney at this time, whose RTWs were being replaced by RTLs. Of note is an antique steam-roller resurfacing the road behind the bus! This RTL was withdrawn when Clapton received RTs late in 1967, and sent to Edmonton for store. It was however reinstated that November at Dalston garage where it survived until replacement by RTs in June 1968. Sold to a dealer in May 1969 and then used as a staff bus by various companies, it was secured for preservation late in 1977 and still exists today.

**Another Clapton** bus, RTL882, calls at Essex Road station on a gloomy 27 December 1965 – my eighteenth birthday! This Metro-Cammell-bodied RTL went for scrap in January 1965, after store in Loughton garage for several months following withdrawal. Trolleybus replacement route 277 would lose its RTLs in favour of RTs between September and December 1967.

**On the** same day, Dalston RTL1610, seen at route 47's Shoreditch Church terminus, is one of the 100 RTLs overhauled again in the latter half of 1965. It would move to West Ham for a final three months when replaced by RTs at Dalston in June 1968, but perished amid the mass withdrawals of RTLs on 'Black Saturday', 7 September 1968. It finally went for scrap in December 1969.

**Also on** 27/12/65, Dalston RTW379 heads a line-up of two others and an RM on the 11's stand outside Broad Street station. Six weeks later, scenes like this would be no more when RMs took over route 11 too. This RTW joined its fellows in Ceylon in December 1966.

**On this** grey December day, Camberwell Metro-Cammell-bodied RTL802 stands at Aldgate bus station on the short 42 route, one of two that crosses Tower Bridge. Following replacement by RTs in the summer of 1966, this RTL was sold for use as members' transport for a bingo club in Buckinghamshire in January 1967, then used briefly by a coach operator in Slough before going for scrap early in 1969.

**The other** route crossing Tower Bridge is the 78, on which at this period Dalston garage worked a small allocation of RTLs alongside Peckham RTs. Around the corner in Minories, their RTL164 is seen, also on 27/12/65. Transferred to Hackney towards the end of 1967, this RTL also perished on 'Black Saturday', 7/9/68, and went for scrap in May 1969.

**The weak** winter sunshine reflects in the windscreen of Chalk Farm RTW182 at Elephant & Castle on 28/12/65. This was one of the last survivors at the garage and would perish on 1 January 1966 when route 45 converted to RM. It languished in store for the whole of 1966 prior to being sold to Ceylon at the end of that year.

**The end** is nigh for Walworth's RTWs too. RTW230 is seen at the Elephant on the same day, three days before RTLs took over all workings on the 176. This one shared the same fate as RTW182, being exported to Ceylon also in December 1966.

**A handful** of RTWs survived at Hackney garage for a few weeks after those at nearby Dalston. One of these was RTW352, seen at Bloomsbury to where it has worked a 'short' from Putney Common on 19/2/66, immediately before its withdrawal and replacement by RTLs. Reconditioned for sale to Ceylon, it never actually got there, and was instead sold to the Yorkshire dealer W. North's in August that year for possible resale.

By **4/3/66**, Brixton was the only garage still operating RTWs, and their RTW152 seen here loading up on route 109 on Westminster Bridge was the only KLB-registered example left in service, having last been overhauled as long ago as October 1960. This one did, however, make it to Ceylon, being sold there in December 1966.

**Tram replacement** route 196 had been all-RTL operated until the autumn of 1965, when those at Highgate garage were replaced by RTs. Now, when RTL1576 was seen in Kingsway on 8/3/66, those at Camberwell were due for replacement by them too. This particular RTL did not enter service until the spring of 1958, and was only overhauled once, in March 1962, with body No.9150 which had been new to RTL1580. It saw a few months' further service at Stonebridge Park when displaced by RTs at Camberwell in the summer of 1966, and was eventually one of the very last RTLs to be sold to Ceylon, in December 1968.

**One that** got away! Very few RTWs were sold for further use in the London area, but an exception was RTW130. It was sold in February 1966 to Stratford building contractor Ford & Walton Ltd, and is seen in their light blue livery in Jessam Avenue, Clapton on 15/3/66. It had last seen service at Walworth garage late in 1965.

**Standing in** for an RM on route 6A, Hackney RTL1398 is seen in Waterloo's Cornwall Road bus park in the company of RM2200 on 24/3/66. This RTL had in fact come to Hackney from Chalk Farm late in 1965 as a replacement for RTWs on routes 22 and 106, and during the summer of 1967 was transferred to Hounslow as a staff bus, yet actually used there briefly in service to cover a shortage of RTs. Withdrawn in November that year, it went for scrap two years later.

**Next day**, 25/3/66, Brixton RTW292 loads up at Addington Street, Waterloo in the shadow of County Hall. The driver of this 109 has forgotten to change his blind from when it reached Blackfriars to run around the Embankment loop. Seven weeks later, the last RTWs would be withdrawn. This one was yet another to be sold to Ceylon in December 1966.

**Brixton's other** RTW route at the end was the 95. Here, on 28/4/66, less than three weeks before the end, their RTW8 is seen in Newington Causeway approaching the Elephant. This RTW was one of the very last of its class to receive an overhaul, in April 1962 and was yet another to go to Ceylon in December 1966. Note the bomb-site on the left, still unrebuilt nearly twenty-five years after the blitz of 10 May 1941 that destroyed so much of this area.

**Also in** Newington Causeway, Metro-Cammell RTL642 is working from Brixton garage and it too will soon be ousted by RTs. For some reason, when Brixton lost its RTs in 1963/64, routes 95 and 109 (along with the Sunday 57A and 95A) were given RTWs, but the 133 had RTLs. These too were on their way out by now. This one, in fact, had already been withdrawn at Walworth but for some reason was reinstated at Brixton in April 1966. It was withdrawn again when RTs replaced Brixton's last RTLs and RTWs in May, and went for scrap in January 1967.

**On Saturday**, 7/5/66, Victoria, Gillingham Street's RTL1180 has apparently been abandoned outside the railway station around the corner when working route 52. Its driver and conductor are probably getting a cup of tea in the crew facilities just out of the picture on the right. Route 52 was shared by Victoria and Willesden garages at this period, and converted to RM operation in the autumn of 1966. However Willesden RTLs still substituted for them right up to the very end two years later. This RTL moved to Bow garage when Victoria's share of route 10 was transferred there at the end of 1966 and withdrawn the following spring. Eventually, it was one of the last RTLs to be sent to Ceylon, in December 1968.

**In the** yard of Gillingham Street garage itself, Battersea roofbox RTL172 takes its break working route 39. RTLs had replaced RTWs on this route, along with the 22 and 31 at Battersea in the autumn of 1965, only to be ousted by RTs in the spring of 1967. It then moved to Clapton garage until also displaced there by RTs in the autumn, and finally for a short while to Hackney where it was withdrawn in November. After being stripped for spares for Ceylon at Stonebridge Park, it went for scrap in April 1969.

**Just around** the corner in Vauxhall Bridge Road, Walworth RTL73 is another of the 23 roofbox RTLs created upon overhaul in 1964 and works tram replacement route 185 which terminates there. This former tram depot lost its RTLs in the autumn of 1966, but this example moved to the East, first to Clapton and then a year later to West Ham, remaining there until the holocaust of 'Black Saturday', 7 September 1968, when the long-delayed first stage of London Transport's ill-fated 'Reshaping Plan' released sufficient RTs to replace all RTLs in the East End. It then spent the best part of a year in store at Grays garage before going for scrap in November 1969.

**By 19/5/66**, Camberwell garage was starting to receive RTs to replace its large allocation of RTLs on routes 35, 42, 59A, 159, 159A, 172 and 196. Here, RTL1583 loads up in Parliament Street on route 59A. Overhauled in September 1965, as one of the extra 100 RTLs done to cover shortages, it moved on to Willesden garage and remained there until the very last day of RTL operation at the end of November 1968. It went for scrap a year later.

**Route 30** had converted to RM operation in the summer of 1964, but RTLs from Hackney garage could be seen on it substituting for RMs for the next four years. Thus on 20/5/66 we see their RTL1585 in the evening rush hour at St. Pancras. This was another of the 100 RTLs given an extra overhaul in 1965, in fact one of the last of these to be outshopped in January 1966. Transferred to Poplar as a result of route 22's conversion to RM in November 1967, it nevertheless perished on 'Black Saturday', 7 September 1968, then gathered dust languishing in store in Poplar until going for scrap in February 1970.

**Seen on** the same occasion, Stockwell Metro-Cammell RTL918 is running back to its garage on route weekday 77A, which was shared with Merton RTs. After withdrawal in the winter of 1966/67, this RTL was sold as a staff bus to a company in Staines in November 1967, but within eighteen months had found its way to the Yorkshire scrapyards.

**By 28/5/66**, replacement of RTLs at Camberwell garage by RTs was well underway, but their RTL1401 still manages to put in an appearance on Saturday-only route 159A when seen here in Parliament Street. Shortly afterwards, it was transferred to West Ham, where it stayed until withdrawal in June 1968. It went for scrap in May 1969.

**Representing the** surviving RTWs on driver training duties at this period, RTW433 is also based at Camberwell, and seen at Parliament Square. Buses of this class were never based there in service, though were used on routes 45, 176, 176A and 185 at the former Walworth tram depot just across the road. It was retired from training duties in January 1970, and went for scrap in December that year.

**Seen on** 3/6/66 beneath the trees at Clapham Common station, Camberwell RTL1223 will soon be a memory, too, as it works a short journey to the Elephant on the long route 35, which at this period was shared with Leyton RTs. Moved to Clapton, where it served until the spring of 1967, it eventually was sold to Ceylon in July 1968.

On the same day, Stockwell RTL731 waits at the traffic lights opposite Stockwell Station, near its home garage, bound for Golders Green on route 2A. Already many of these 450 Metro-Cammell-bodied RTLs had been withdrawn, and now the RTWs had gone; the process was speeded up – all were withdrawn within a year, by which time all RTLs at Stockwell were being replaced by RTs, or in the case of the 2 group of routes, RMs. This one was withdrawn when RMs replaced RTLs on route 2B in the autumn of 1966, and sold to Yorkshire dealers W. North's in February 1967, being scrapped a few months later.

At Golders Green itself already on 4/6/66, another Metro-Cammell-bodied RTL, Cricklewood's RTL804, lays over on route 2 while its crew take a break in the canteen on the Northern Line station, shared at the time by London Transport bus and Underground staff before that wonderful organisation was wrecked by the Thatcher regime, somewhat appropriately in the year 1984! The RTL stands in the turning circle built for trolleybuses, and it is a matter of opinion whether it really will work a 'short' from here to North Finchley, or whether it has been curtailed from working there. Route 2 converted to RM operation in the summer of 1967, but Cricklewood retained RTLs on routes 142 and 240, the latter also working to Golders Green, until the end of October 1968. This one, however, was withdrawn a few weeks after this picture was taken, and was dumped outside its garage until being moved to Stonebridge Park three years later and going for scrap in October 1969.

**Another Metro**-Cammell-bodied RTL seen at Golders Green bus station that day is RTL902, working from Wandsworth garage on route 28. Those that worked this route from Middle Row garage had already gone in the autumn of 1965, and those at this former tram and trolleybus depot would follow during the winter of 1966/67, all replaced by RTs. Following withdrawal, this one was sent initially to Loughton garage for mechanical work prior to sale to Ceylon, where it eventually arrived in July 1968.

**An unusual** fate for one of the Metro-Cammell-bodied RTLs befell RTL768, the first of its batch to be sold by London Transport. It went initially in July 1965 to a dealer, F. Tendler of Whitton, Middlesex and then the following month to London independent operator Seth Coaches of Kentish Town for spare parts. It is seen dumped in their yard on 5/6/66, not only stripped of mechanical parts, but also having lost its front roof dome, which was fitted to Seth's Park Royal-bodied RT759 after an accident! RTL768 had itself been withdrawn in 1964 following an accident when in service at Camberwell garage, and also been cannibalised at Aldenham prior to disposal.

By **14/6/66**, few RTLs were left at Camberwell garage, but one of the last survivors there was roofbox RTL1438, seen heading north along Upper Street towards Highbury Corner on my local tram-replacement route 172. It would be resettled in the East at Poplar after being ousted by RTs, but would perish on 'Black Saturday', 7 September 1968 in common with all other RTLs in the East End. It is interesting to look at the bus routes shown on the bus stop flag – the 43 (weekdays), 104 (daily), 133 (Sunday), 172 (weekdays), 188A (Sundays) and 279 (daily), along with night route N92. All of these ran along Upper Street from Islington, Angel, then along Holloway Road to the Nag's Head. Nearly fifty years later, only ONE bus route does this – the daily, 24-hour route 43! Night route N41 serves these roads too. Meanwhile, the unfortunate RTL1438 had made its last journey to the Yorkshire scrapyards in May 1969.

On **18/6/66**, Metro-Cammell-bodied RTLs 691 and 914 head a group of their fellows in the yard of Cricklewood garage. Their days are now numbered, though route 60 would survive with standard RTLs until withdrawal on 'Black Saturday', 7 September 1968. Both were withdrawn before 1966 was out, being sold to Yorkshire dealers in January and November 1967 respectively and subsequently scrapped.

**Seen on** the same day, Metro-Cammell RTL646 had been one of the first of these vehicles to be sold for further use in Britain, initially to P.V.S. (dealers) of Upminster and then, in October 1965, to Isleworth Coaches, who took over operation of London Transport route 235 between Richmond station and Richmond Hill in February 1966. However, on this occasion, the RTL is joined by one of its companions to take the 'desperate and the gullible' (as many in the British press called them at the time) to the American evangelist Billy Graham's 'crusade' at Earl's Court. Note how this one has merely had its London Transport fleet name and legal ownership panel painted over, but still shows its bonnet plate number! Isleworth sold it on in the spring of 1968 to an operator in Slough, who used it for a few more years.

**The well**-known Nottinghamshire independent operator Barton of Chilwell purchased several RTLs from London Transport, and here at Ilkeston, RTL1486 has recently become this operator's No.1042 when seen on 26/6/66. This operator's smart red, cream and dark brown livery particularly suited the RTLs. This one had come via P.V.S. (dealers) in January 1966, and had last worked for London Transport at West Ham garage, being withdrawn and sold for scrap by Barton in September 1968, by coincidence the same month that its old home, West Ham garage, lost its RTLs.

When it lost its trolleybuses in January 1962, Stonebridge Park depot gained a small allocation of RTLs on route 112 from Cricklewood garage, in exchange for RM workings on former trolleybus route 266. These would eventually be some of the last RTLs of all in service, succumbing to RTs at the end of October 1968, when this one was withdrawn. It remained dumped there, where it was cannibalised for spare parts for Ceylon, until going for scrap in June 1969. All that is in the future, as a smart RTL1433 is seen on 2/7/66 on this long route, then running all the way around the North Circular Road from Palmers Green to Ealing, near the garage. Note the young lad on the right, still in short trousers, clutching his bus-spotting note book, who, when he saw me photograph the RTL, told me he had just been ejected from Stonebridge Park garage! I wonder where he is today?

Following the replacement of the last RTLs at Camberwell garage by RTs in June 1966, attentions now shifted across the road to Walworth, which began to receive RTs to replace theirs at the beginning of July. On 9/7/66, smart RTL1599, which had been overhauled in November 1965 as one of the extra 100 RTLs done late that year, awaits departure for Greenwich on tram replacement route 185's Vauxhall Bridge Road stand. Sent to Stonebridge Park for route 112 from Walworth, it shared the same fate as RTL1433, above, being withdrawn at the end of October 1968, cannibalised for spares for Ceylon and then sent for scrap a year later.

**On 12/7/66**, RTL1624, one of the last batch of RTLs which did not enter service until the spring of 1958, lays over at Aldgate bus station on the busy 25. This one was one of several that were overhauled only once, in this case gaining Park Royal body No.3781 which had been new to RTL542 in 1950, so at least the body had had some sixteen years' use when it was withdrawn in the winter of 1966/67. It spent most of 1967 in store before being sold to Ceylon that December. Route 25, of course, kept its large allocation of RTLs until 'Black Saturday', 7 September 1968.

**As mentioned** earlier, over half of the 500-strong RTW fleet was exported to Ceylon, whilst most of the 150 or so that were used as driver trainers eventually went straight for scrap when their services were no longer needed. Therefore, not very many were sold for further use in Britain. One that was, however, was RTW26. A late survivor at Brixton garage, it was sold in June 1966 to Pocknell's Viola Coaches of Dulwich, and is seen soon afterwards in their smart maroon livery in Waterloo Road car park on 14/7/66. Note the name 'Viola' has been painted over its London Transport radiator badge!

**On 23/7/66,** Wandsworth RTL1149 glints in the sun while awaiting departure from Golders Green bus station on route 28. Both its front advertisements and the C.N.D. graffiti daubed on the 'gents' behind it reflect what is now referred to as the 'Cold War hysteria' of the period! Wandsworth garage would lose its RTLs in the winter of 1966/67 to RT replacement too. This one moved to Bow, from where it was withdrawn in the spring of 1967. It joined the hundreds of other RTLs and RTWs in Ceylon in July 1968.

**Few RTLs** remained at Walworth garage when their Metro-Cammell RTL941 was seen on a Saturday lunchtime journey on route 185 in Vauxhall Bridge Road on 30/7/66. Unusually, it became a driver trainer at Mortlake garage for a few months after being ousted by RTs at Walworth, eventually being sold to Ceylon in August 1968. Of the bus routes shown on this terminal bus stop, the 50 (weekdays), 57A (Sundays), 181 (weekdays) and 185 (daily) – all tram replacement routes or derivatives thereof – only the 185 still serves this point today.

**Just around** the corner in Wilton Road, sister Metro-Cammell RTL939 is seen working from Stockwell garage on route 2B. This was the first of the 2 group of routes to receive RMs, in the autumn of 1966, whereupon this RTL was withdrawn. More than two years later, it was one of the last RTLs to be sold to Ceylon, in December 1968. Note the adverts for 'Southern Service' on the wall of Victoria station. This relates to the Southern Region of British Railways, which was a public service at the time, unlike today when train services are privatised and geared to gain their owners fat profits!

**Though looking** no different from the two Metro-Cammell-bodied RTLs seen above, Stockwell's RTL1005 is in fact an oddity. This carries the body of that type left over at Aldenham when their final overhauls ceased in the autumn of 1965 following the overhaul of RTL626 with a standard, Park Royal body early in 1962. It was therefore outshopped as the nearest stocknumber available to the MCCW batch (RTL450-RTL1000). This view sees it working one of the Saturday afternoon short journeys between Victoria and West Norwood, Rosendale and laying over on the stand in Vauxhall Bridge Road, also on 30/7/66. Withdrawn early in 1967, it too went to Ceylon in November of that year.

**Also on** 30/7/66 – the day of the World Cup Final in which England beat West Germany – a very smart Willesden RTL1583 picks up passengers in Waterloo Road on that garage's Saturday-only allocation on route 1. One of the 100 RTLs given extra overhauls in late 1965, it had initially been sent to Camberwell garage, moving to Willesden a few weeks before this picture was taken. It was one of the very last RTLs in service when withdrawn at the end of November 1968, and sadly went for scrap a year later.

**At this** period, Stockwell garage had a few duties on weekend route 77B. On Sunday, 31/7/66, smart RTL543, another of those overhauled in the autumn of 1965, stands at Euston Square. Moved to Cricklewood when route 2B lost RTLs a couple of months later, it then moved on to Willesden in the summer of 1967. It would also become one of the very last RTLs in service at the end of November 1968, but would go for scrap a year later, too.

**On 4/8/66**, Metro-Cammell-bodied RTL988 is seen on tram replacement route 168 in Parliament Street working from Wandsworth garage, which shared this route with Stockwell. Several of this type were still there at this time, though all were swept away by the time Wandsworth lost their last RTLs in February 1967. This particular one was exported to Jersey where it joined several other RTLs with Jersey Motor Transport in April that year, and it saw some six years' service on the island. It was later returned to mainland Britain and preserved.

**Another of** the last 100 RTLs to be overhauled, RTL1529 is seen on Walworth's share of the 176 in Waterloo Road, also on 4/8/66. Moved to Wandsworth when this garage lost RTLs a few weeks later, it then moved again to Stockwell after Wandsworth followed suit. And then when Stockwell lost their RTLs in the summer of 1967, it was sent to West Ham where it remained until withdrawn on 'Black Saturday', 7 September 1968. It was another to spend most of 1969 in store at Grays, going for scrap in November that year.

**On a** sunny Tuesday, 16/8/66, Stockwell Metro-Cammell RTL927 heads for Raynes Park on weekday route 77A when seen in Parliament Street. For some reason, this one languished in store, most of that time in Fulwell garage, for three years after withdrawal before going for scrap in October 1969.

**On the** same day, Walworth RTL1336 pulls away from the stop in Addington Street, Waterloo on tram replacement route 184, now rapidly being converted to RT operation. This RTL carried a very late body, No.9143, which had been new to RTL1573, which perhaps explains why it survived to be transferred to Cricklewood garage, where it survived until the spring of 1967, five years after its last (and the body's only) overhaul. It eventually was sold to Ceylon, in April 1968.

**Not far** away, outside St. Thomas's Hospital next day, 17/8/66, Wandsworth Metro-Cammell RTL881 heads for its home town on tram replacement route 170. Withdrawn when replaced by RTs during the coming winter, this RTL was eventually one of the last exported to Ceylon, some two years later in December 1968.

**Route 44** was also a tram replacement route operated by Wandsworth garage and had in fact also replaced their sole trolleybus route, the 612, back in October 1950, reviving the former routeing of the 12 tram all the way from London Bridge station to Mitcham. Here, also on 17/8/66, RTL319 calls at Lambeth Palace on the last leg of the long journey to London Bridge. This RTL never ran again in London after being ousted by RTs at Wandsworth early in 1967, spending the rest of that year and nearly all of 1968 being prepared for export to Ceylon, to where it was sold in December 1968 as one of the very last to go there.

**Next day**, 18/8/66, Walworth Metro-Cammell-bodied RTL568 calls at Lambeth North station on its way to Forest Hill on tram replacement route 171, which was shared with Tottenham garage. RTLs from that garage lasted on this route until mid-June 1968, but by now, those at Walworth had just a few weeks left. This one was used briefly as a trainer at Southall garage after withdrawal, eventually being yet another to reach Ceylon, in this case in November 1967.

**On the** same day, I was lucky to catch this shot of Dalston RTL1432 escorting an RM on route 11 at the traffic lights at the southern end of Parliament Street. RTLs based at this garage continued to substitute for RMs on the busy 11 right up to their replacement by RTs on routes 47 and 78 there in June 1968. This one survived in service until that time, languishing in store after that until finally going for scrap in January 1970.

**In the** yard of Victoria, Gillingham Street garage on 2/9/66, Bow's roofbox RTL247 on route 10 makes an interesting contrast with an XA class Leyland Atlantean on route 76. The RTL was transferred to Clapton when Bow-operated route 26 was withdrawn at the end of the year, then withdrawn as a result of that garage receiving RTs in November 1967. Having worked firstly for an independent operator in Norfolk after sale in August 1968 and then subsequently being exported to be used as a tourist bus on the island of Sentosa, it ended up on the seabed off the shore of that island as a breeding ground for fish in the early 1980s!

**Next day**, 3/9/66, Dalston roofbox RTL143 calls at Bromley garage on its long journey from Farnborough to Shoreditch on route 47. This remained in service there until RTs replaced Dalston's RTLs in mid-June 1968, then went for scrap in May 1969.

**Some RTW** driver trainers were housed at Country Area garages, where they had never been based when in service. This explains why RTW319, seen in the yard of Hertford garage on 9/9/66, carries advertisements for Green Rovers! It was in fact officially allocated to Cricklewood garage, as the W code shows, being finally withdrawn from Brixton in January 1970 and sold for scrap in March 1971.

**At Victoria** bus station on 21/9/66, West Ham RTL229 makes an imposing sight working a 25 'short' to Forest Gate, Green Street. Note the 'patriotic' advertisements on the front, inspired by the foreign exchange crisis then being suffered by Harold Wilson's Labour government! Moved to Poplar a few months later, this RTL remained there until withdrawal on 'Black Saturday', 7 September 1968.

**Walworth garage** finally lost their last RTLs on 1 October 1966. One of them, roofbox RTL141, has been transferred to Stockwell and when seen in the evening rush hour at Charing Cross station on 6/10/66 appears not to have had a correct set of blinds fitted for route 77A! This one moved on to Clapton when Stockwell's RTLs were also replaced by RTs in the summer of 1967, only to be withdrawn there in November that year. It was sold to Ceylon in August 1968.

**Another of** the relatively few RTWs sold for domestic use was RTW413, which went to Super Coaches of Upminster in April 1966. It looks smart in their blue and cream livery when seen on an Omnibus Touring Circle outing outside Red Rover of Aylesbury's depot on 16/10/66. This RTW was experimentally fitted with pneumocyclic semi-automatic transmission, as previously on RTW375 (which had carried its body, No.3289 prior to final overhaul). Later used on contract to Lesney's of Hackney Wick as a staff bus, it finally went for scrap in October 1970.

**Red Rover** had had a number of ex-London Transport RT types since the 1950s, starting with a Craven-bodied RT. They also had an RTW, RTW124 which is seen here at their depot, bearing their dark red and cream livery. They acquired it in March 1965, and it was withdrawn in October 1970, being broken up for spare parts thereafter.

**RTL358, seen** here in the company of a 3RT3 the same day, with a dome that has lost many 'arguments' with low trees, had a much longer career with Red Rover, being bought by them in July 1959 and withdrawn in January 1973. After passing through a number of owners, ranging from preservationists to church groups, it has in recent years been secured for preservation.

**Also on** 16/10/66, RTW456 is seen in the maroon livery of Buckmaster of Leighton Buzzard, who had acquired it in June of that year. Sold to a showman in April 1968, it survived for a couple of years in fairground use. The other RTW in this view at Buckmaster's depot is RTW497, which happily survives in preservation today.

**On a** wet Thursday, 20/10/66 at Chiswick Works, RTW10 has been in use as the permanent skid bus, kept there to instruct trainee drivers how to handle a bus if it skids on wet surfaces. This RTW had recently been repainted and given a grey waistband, the only one so adorned at the time, until the majority of driver trainers were likewise treated in 1968. It was retired from this role in May 1969 and sold for scrap in November that year.

**Leaving Chiswick** Works on the same occasion, RTL952 is one of a small number of Metro-Cammell-bodied RTLs used on training duties during 1966/67, and is allocated to Mortlake garage. It was sold to Ceylon in July 1968.

**Seen on** 21/10/66 outside Clapton garage in Mare Street, Hackney, RTL1010 is running the short distance from the 22's traditional Homerton terminus to its home garage, Hackney, in Well Street, probably owing to a staff cut. This RTL will soon be withdrawn and carries body No.9220, built by Weymann for RTL1625 late in 1954 and only ever overhauled once, in May 1962, owing to the bus not having entered service until the spring of 1958. It was sold to Ceylon in May 1968. When I took this photograph, I had no idea that I would be working as a conductor on route 22 eight years later, though from Clapton garage and only on RMs.

**At the** same spot, Clapton RTL1193 has deposited its last passengers and is about to run in, also probably as a result of a staff cut. Its blind shows 'Hackney Station', implying that it has run from Finsbury Park on route 106. Buses terminating here from the south (or west) showed the destination 'Hackney, Clarence Road', which was where the last passengers were set down on the one-way system here. Ridiculously, the station had been closed in 1944 due to wartime bombing, not to reopen (as Hackney Central) until 1980! Today, it is part of the busy and hugely successful London Overground network. As for RTL1193, it had moved to Clapton from Camberwell a few months previously, was withdrawn in the summer of 1967, and sold to Ceylon in July 1968.

**Also on** 21/10/66, RTL415 runs out from Bow garage on route 25, which was one of the RTL class's final strongholds. It is seen at the junction of Fairfield Road and Bow Road. Overhauled to Bow in September 1964, it spent exactly four years there until withdrawn on 'Black Saturday', 7 September 1968. Sadly, after that no one wanted it and it went for scrap in June 1969.

Around the corner at Blackwall Tunnel route 108's Bow, Seven Stars terminus, Poplar RTL1556 sets off for that route's weekday terminus at Lower Sydenham. This was one of the 100 extra RTLs overhauled in late 1965, being sent to Poplar in August of that year. Although also withdrawn on 'Black Saturday', 7 September 1968, this was one of few RTLs whose service lives ended that day which was not scrapped. It was sold to a catering company, with whom it spent some eight years. The 'Danger, Road Works Ahead' notice in the background refers to the Greater London Council's awful Bow Bridge Flyover then being built by the department I worked for at County Hall.

At this period, Poplar garage also worked weekday route 56, which performed a loop around the Isle of Dogs, running from Blackwall Tunnel to Limehouse. Here, roofbox RTL68 arrives at its Limehouse terminus. This was the first of the twenty-three RTLs overhauled with these bodies in 1964, to appear in January of that year, and the lowest-numbered. Withdrawn late in 1967, it was sold in July 1968, initially to West London independent operator White City Coaches. It passed into preservation in the early 1970s, actually being hired back to London Transport to cover for a shortage of RTs on driver training duties in the summer of 1978. It was then exported in 1993 to New Zealand, where it is still going strong as this book is put together in the spring of 2015!

**Another Docklands** route operated by Poplar's RTLs was the 82, running through the Rotherhithe Tunnel and around Surrey Commercial Docks. This view finds Metro-Cammell-bodied RTL944, now due for imminent withdrawal, lurking beneath the bridges of Stepney East Station (today renamed Limehouse) at the route's northern terminus. This RTL was exported to Ceylon in April 1968, six months before route 82 was withdrawn without replacement.

**RTLs from** both Poplar and West Ham garages worked contract services for the Port of London Authority for dock workers. These actually ran within the bonded areas of the Royal Docks and were therefore not available to members of the public and so did not carry route numbers. Here, also on 21/10/66, Poplar RTL417 awaits its crew at Blackwall Tunnel, Northern Approach and unfortunately shows blank blinds instead of the special PLA display it should have had. A year later, this RTL suffered premature withdrawal as a result of an accident, but it remained in stock to be cannibalised for spare parts for Ceylon at Stonebridge Park, prior to eventually going for scrap in April 1969.

Over on the other side of London on 22/10/66, RTL1298 attracts the attention of a point inspector at the Shepherd's Bush Green terminus of route 49. By now, Battersea RTLs only had a small allocation on this route on Saturdays alongside the daily Merton and Streatham RTs, and this ceased at the end of December. Ousted by RTs at Battersea in the spring of 1967, this RTL moved on to Poplar for a few more months. It was sold for use as a staff bus by a firm in Waltham Abbey in February 1968, and then worked school contracts for Ward's Coaches of Epping between 1969 and 1974. Loaned by them for a few weeks in the latter year to National Bus Company fleet Aldervalley to cover vehicle shortages, it was sold initially for preservation in 1975, but ended up being 'bombed' in a scene from the Second World War film featuring the London blitz three years later!

Not many former London Transport RTLs saw use with British municipal fleets, but a handful did with Walsall Corporation. On 23/10/66, former RTL1494 is seen in their light blue livery as their No.205, beneath the trolleybus wires in the town centre. Acquired by them in August 1959, it went for scrap in February 1968. In this view, a couple of Walsall trolleybuses may just be glimpsed in the background.

**On 29/10/66**, Stockwell RTL1047 stands at the Tally Ho! North Finchley bus station terminus of route 2, working a Saturday journey to Norwood garage. This RTL was withdrawn when routes 2 and 2A received RMs in the summer of 1967 and was sold to Ceylon in December that year.

**A grey** and misty morning rush hour of Friday, 25/11/66 sees Hackney RTL1018 substituting for an RM on route 30 at Islington, Angel. Of note in this view is Stone's electrical shop's 'Terrific Sale' aimed at fleecing the gullible in time for Christmas before they went bankrupt! RTL1018 was another of the extra 100 RTLs overhauled in the latter part of 1965, sent initially that December to nearby Clapton. For some reason it went into store at Edmonton late in 1967, but was reinstated to Bow garage in January 1968, moving down the road to Poplar the following month. Inevitably, it perished there on 'Black Saturday', 7 September 1968, languishing in store at its former garage until going for scrap in February 1970.

**Notwithstanding route** 37 having been one of the first RT/RTL-operated routes to convert to RM in December 1962 (and then to RML in the summer of 1966), Stockwell RTLs still had a number of duties on the route on Saturdays until RMs from route 2's conversion enabled their replacement in the spring of 1967. Here, on 17/12/66, their RTL1107 loads up with Christmas shoppers in downtown Brixton. This RTL was withdrawn at the time of the 2's conversion, ending up as one of the last to be sold to Ceylon in December 1968. Once again, local shops may be seen trying to take advantage of 'Christmas goodwill'!

**On the** same day as the previous picture, Battersea RTL968 departs from busy route 31's Chelsea, Stanley Arms terminus. Although by now only a handful of these Metro-Cammell-bodied RTLs remained in service, now fewer than three of them still running from Battersea garage turned up here on the 31 on this occasion! All were withdrawn following route cuts at the end of the month, but saw further use for a few months as staff buses. This one ended up at the Stonebridge Park dump being cannibalised for spares for Ceylon, finally going for scrap in April 1969. Note in this picture the cafe and adjacent betting shop on the right, which appear to be popular with bus crews!

**Also at** Chelsea, Stanley Arms that day, Battersea RTL112 has turned short on route 22 as one of the Metro-Cammell-bodied RTLs on the 31 referred to above stands behind it. Moved on to Clapton when Battersea lost its RTLs in the spring of 1967, it was withdrawn towards the end of the year and sold to Ceylon in December 1968.

**Next day**, 18/12/66, Clapton RTL1345 is seen at Victoria station working their Sunday allocation on route 38A to distant Loughton. Its body, No.9144, was new to RTL1574, another that did not enter service until the spring of 1958 and which, therefore, was only overhauled once, in January 1962. Now due for early withdrawal, this RTL was sold to Ceylon in October 1967.

**It is** Friday, 30/12/66, and the last day of trolleybus replacement route 26. Here, at Aldgate bus station, Bow Metro-Cammell-bodied RTL571 awaits departure for Leyton. This RTL was withdrawn as a result of the 26's demise, and was eventually sold to Ceylon two years later.

**To compensate** Bow for the loss of route 26, duties on route 10 which had been shared with Victoria (Gillingham Street) garage were transferred there. Here we see Victoria's RTL1557 working it on their last day, also at Aldgate. Transferred to Cricklewood garage as a result, from where it was withdrawn during the summer of 1967, this RTL was sold in August 1968 to a film company, with whom it appeared in Hammer Horror films *Quatermass and the Pit* and *Son of Jack the Ripper*, the latter being filmed in the Aldgate area. It was finally burnt out in an episode of the TV series *On The Buses*.

**Another route** withdrawn at the end of December 1966 was the 256A, a Saturday-only service that had been introduced in January 1964 which replaced parts of routes 256 and 257, running from Chingford Mount to London Bridge. It was shared between Walthamstow RMs and Clapton RTLs. One of the latter, RTL1237, is seen in Norton Folgate on the last day, 30/12/66. Withdrawn in the summer of 1967, this RTL was dumped at the rear of Walthamstow garage until going for scrap in May 1969.

**Also on** 30/12/66, Willesden's roofbox RTL1328 stands at the Harlesden, Willesden Junction Hotel terminus of route 226. Although, along with the 176, this would be the last London Transport route to operate RTLs at the end of November 1968, this one did not last that long, being transferred to Cricklewood garage shortly after this picture was taken, and then to Bow in April 1968. It perished on 'Black Saturday', 7 September that year, finally going for scrap also in May 1969.

Route 73's large allocation of RTLs was replaced by RMs in early December 1962, after which they were very seldom seen on this busy route. However on 7 January 1967, Tottenham RTL294 has put in an appearance, and is seen at a gloomy Euston Square. Note the point inspector chatting to its conductor: perhaps the slower RTL cannot keep pace with the newer RMs, and has been curtailed at East Sheen instead of going through to Richmond. This RTL was withdrawn in the autumn of 1967 and sold to Ceylon in August 1968.

On a crisp, sunny 8th January 1967, Clapton RTL1198 calls at Essex Road station on its way to Victoria, working their Sunday allocation of the 38A. The bus seems remarkably full for a winter Sunday, perhaps taking passengers to Islington's Chapel Market which was then open on Sunday mornings. The body on this RTL, No.9193, had been new to RTL1569 which did not enter service until the spring of 1958. It was overhauled only once, when outshopped as RTL1198 in July 1962, and withdrawn in the spring of 1967, being sold to Ceylon in April 1968.

**On 11** January 1967, Battersea RTL1572 on route 19 has taken me part of the way to work, from Islington Town Hall to Holborn Station, where it waits at the traffic lights on the one-way system to cross Kingsway. From here, a 68, 188 or 196 would take me to the South Bank and my job at County Hall. Carrying body No.9154 which had been new to RTL1584, this RTL was last overhauled in January 1962 and due for imminent withdrawal and, once again, the body had only had the one overhaul having not entered service until the spring of 1958. Withdrawn shortly after this picture was taken, RTL1572 was sold to P.V.S. (dealers) in August 1967, and exported to the USA in December. Used as a restaurant in Boston, it was unfortunately badly vandalised in 1970 and scrapped soon afterwards.

**Route 9** had converted from RTL to RM operation in the summer of 1963, after which appearances of RTLs on the route (from Dalston garage, which still had some for routes 47 and 78) were quite rare. Here, however, on 19 January 1967, their RTL1313 is seen at Aldwych at lunchtime on its way from Mortlake to Liverpool Street. Odd appearances could still be made on this route, and the 11, until Dalston's RTLs were replaced by RTs in June 1968. This one lasted until then, and eventually went for scrap in May 1969.

**Just around** the corner on 20/1/67, Hackney RTL1611 stands in for an RML on route 6A and is about to cross Waterloo Bridge. This was one of the very last RTLs to be overhauled, coming off Aldenham's 'works float' in January 1966 when overhauling of the 100 extra RTLs taken in during the latter half of 1965 ended. It had actually been sent to Hackney to replace some of the last RTWs there on routes 22 and 106. For some reason it was transferred to Bow in March 1968, where it perished on 'Black Saturday', 7 September 1968. It was then stored unwanted in Finchley garage until going for scrap in February 1970.

**At Waterloo** itself, RTL1336 arrives on route 60 with blinds already set for its return journey to Cricklewood garage. Having last been overhauled in February 1962, this was withdrawn shortly after this picture was taken. It carried body No.9143 which only had that one overhaul, having been new to RTL1573 which did not enter service until the spring of 1958. RTL1336 was sold to Ceylon in April 1968, five months before route 60 was withdrawn and replaced by new RM-operated route 8B which ran from Cricklewood to Bloomsbury.

**On 30/1/67**, Willesden RTL1045 is seen outside Waterloo station on route 176. As mentioned earlier, this would be one of the last two routes to operate RTLs in London at the end of November 1968. However, this one was withdrawn later in 1967 and sold to Ceylon in April 1968.

**One of** the 23 roofbox RTLs created upon overhaul in 1964, Battersea RTL246 calls at St. Mary's Church, Upper Street, Islington on 31 January 1967. This garage lost its RTLs between March and June 1967, replaced by RTs, resulting in this one being transferred to West Ham. In common with all other RTLs in the East End, it perished on 'Black Saturday', 7 September 1968. It went for scrap in May 1969.

*An extremely* rare working indeed as dusk falls on Friday, 3 February 1967 is that of Tottenham roofbox RTL98 on route 73 in Euston Road. No RTLs carried this type of body at the time the 73 converted from RTL to RM operation in December 1962. This one has found its way onto the route as a result of XA-class Leyland Atlanteans on route 76 at its garage being notoriously unreliable, resulting in RMs usually used on the 73 having to stand in for them and therefore causing a shortage of the type. Based at Tottenham for route 171, this RTL was withdrawn when that route gained RTs in June 1968 and sold for scrap in May 1969.

**On Saturday**, 4 February 1967, Parliament Street seems very quiet as Stockwell RTL1172 heads for Kings Cross on the weekend 77C route. Withdrawn soon after this picture was taken, this RTL was sold to Ceylon in November 1967.

**Another Stockwell** bus, RTL1230, has just completed its circuit of Euston Square when seen on the weekday 77A on Monday, 6/2/67. Just visible in the background are demolition works that removed Euston station's famous Doric arch. Meanwhile, this RTL was also withdrawn shortly afterwards and sold to Ceylon in November.

**All is** quiet at Stamford Hill Broadway on Saturday, 11 February 1967 as Clapton roofbox RTL1475 performs a short working of route 253A to Hackney, Well Street. This was the highest-numbered roofbox RTL, and when Clapton lost them in the autumn of 1967, it was transferred to Tottenham that November. Withdrawn when RTs replaced them on route 171 in June 1968, it went for scrap the following May.

On 18/2/67, Stockwell RTL1571 has arrived at the Wilton Road, Victoria terminus of tram replacement route 181 and already has its blinds set for the return journey to Streatham garage. This was another of the RTLs that did not enter service until the spring of 1958, having been overhauled only once, in May 1962. It was withdrawn a few days after this picture was taken, and sold to P.V.S. (dealers) in March. Later passing to Barton of Chilwell, it was used by them for just a few months in 1969, going for scrap the following year.

**Upper Street**, Islington is almost deserted as Battersea RTL50 works route 19's Sunday extension from Tooting Bec to Streatham garage early in the morning of 19/2/67. RTLs at Battersea were now due for imminent replacement by RTs, resulting in this one being transferred to Clapton a couple of weeks later. It was then moved on to Poplar when that garage lost its RTLs in the autumn, remaining there until 'Black Saturday', 7 September 1968 when it was withdrawn. It went for scrap in October 1969. Of note are its front adverts which reflect the 'establishment's' paranoia about the antics of the 'pop stars' of the day!

**Numerically the** penultimate RTL, Stockwell RTL1630 escorts an RM on the 11 and another RTL on the 39 around Parliament Square when working route 88 on 20/2/67. This was one of the 100 RTLs overhauled in late 1965, having been outshopped in December that year, and moved to Clapton when Stockwell lost RTLs in the spring of 1967. It was then transferred to Bow when Clapton lost theirs in the autumn, remaining there until the devastating Reshaping Plan changes of 7 September 1968 and its consequent withdrawal. It then languished in store at Poplar until going for scrap in February 1970.

**Next day**, a sunny Tuesday, 21/2/67, Cricklewood RTL1061 leaves Cornwall Road bus park, Waterloo for home. Withdrawn in the spring, it was sold to Ceylon in April 1968.

On Saturday, 4 March 1967, five of Stonebridge Park's allocation of RTLs for route 112 are parked outside the garage. They are, from right to left, RTL439, 266, 1596, 1041 and 1576. Cricklewood and Stonebridge Park were the penultimate garages to lose RTLs, which they did on 26 October 1968, five weeks before the very last went at nearby Willesden. With the exception of RT1576, which was withdrawn in August 1968 and sold to Ceylon the following December, all survived on route 112 until the end, then being dumped at the rear of the garage until going for scrap at various times during 1969, some of them being cannibalised for spares for Ceylon.

On the same occasion as the previous picture, Metro-Cammell-bodied RTL734 has already been in store at Stonebridge Park for several months, following its withdrawal from nearby Willesden garage. Just as was the case with trolleybuses here, the garage yard has become a concentration point for withdrawn RTLs and RTWs. RTL1623 on the right had been there since late 1965! RTL734 and RTL1623 would remain here and be progressively cannibalised for spare parts for Ceylon until going for scrap in May and June 1969 respectively.

**A long** queue of passengers outside Kilburn High Road station board Battersea RTL1121 bound for Camden Town on route 31 on 11/3/67. Withdrawn as a result of RTs arriving at Battersea a few weeks later, this RTL was sold in July 1967 to A1 Services of Ardrossan, Ayrshire, with whom it saw some five years' further service.

**Route 8** had converted from RTW to RM operation early in 1965, but here in the morning rush hour of Wednesday, 15/3/67, Bow RTL342 stands in for an RM when seen in Proctor Street, Holborn. This RTL had recently been transferred there from Wandsworth and would remain at Bow until that fateful day, 7 September 1968 when all RTLs in the East End were withdrawn. It finally went for scrap in May 1969.

**Bow garage** had a large allocation of RTLs for routes 10 and 25. Also on 15/3/67, RTL932 is seen in the company of an RT and an RM at London Bridge station working a short journey of the former to Victoria. This was now one of only three Metro-Cammell-bodied RTLs remaining in service, all of which were at Bow. All had gone by the summer of 1967, this one eventually being one of the last RTLs to go to Ceylon, in December 1968.

**Across the** Thames at Aldgate, West Ham RTL1127 will also soon be withdrawn. It too heads for Victoria, but on the 25 through the West End. Note the BESI (bus electronic scanning indicator) brackets between decks on its front nearside, which were used in an early attempt to dispense with roadside bus inspectors! This RTL went to Ceylon in August 1968.

On **18/3/67**, Stockwell RTL1234 is seen near its home garage working weekend route 77C in Wandsworth Road. Now due for early withdrawal, it would be sold to Ceylon in April 1968.

**Inside Stockwell** garage's cavernous space, RTL1021 and RTL1228 are amongst a group of RTLs that have just been withdrawn as a result of others that had been overhauled more recently being transferred there following replacement by RTs at nearby Battersea garage. Both went to Ceylon, in November and December 1967 respectively.

**For some** reason, a number of Metro-Cammell-bodied RTLs were retained as staff buses at garages in south-west London at this period. One was RTL583, seen within the small Twickenham garage, also on 18/3/67. It appears to be in very good condition, and following final withdrawal a few months later was yet another to make the trip to Ceylon, in July 1968.

**On 20/3/67**, Stockwell RTL429 sets off from Vauxhall Bridge Road, Victoria on route 2. Moved to Clapton when the 2 converted to RM operation in June, this RTL was them transferred to Cricklewood in November 1967. Withdrawn on 'Black Saturday', 7 September 1968, upon the withdrawal of route 60, it was dumped at Stonebridge Park and cannibalised for spares for Ceylon before going for scrap in June 1969.

**Dalston had** a small allocation of RTLs on route 78, alongside a larger allocation of RTs from Peckham garage. On 21/3/67, their RTL1013 escorts one of the latter past Aldgate station, passing a West Ham roofbox RTL which is terminating on route 25. RTL1013 was one of the extra batch overhauled in late 1965, initially arriving at Walworth in December and then moving on to Wandsworth and, early in 1967, Dalston. When that garage lost them in June 1968, it was one of few survivors, since it moved on to West Ham, only to perish in the holocaust of 'Black Saturday', 7 September 1968. It finally went for scrap in December 1969.

Next day, **22/3/67**, West Ham RTL1312 has terminated at Holborn, Red Lion Square from the west, and stands in Proctor Street ready to return to Victoria as a point inspector notes the proceedings! This RTL was unique, in being the only one of the class ever to carry a Weymann roofbox body. The body (No.2260) was, moreover, new to Country Area RT981 and was the only survivor of that batch, all of the others having been sold in 1963/64 when all roofbox RTs in the Country Area were withdrawn. Sent to West Ham for route 25 upon overhaul in November 1964, it remained there until withdrawal on 'Black Saturday', 7 September 1968, and went for scrap in May 1969.

**The RTLs** at Dalston garage for routes 47 and 78 quite often substituted for RMs on route 11. RTL546 does so on 23/3/67 and is seen passing Victoria District Line station. Withdrawn shortly after this picture was taken, for some reason it languished in store in Dalston garage until December 1969, finally going for scrap two months later.

**On the** same day, RTL341 stands outside Victoria, Gillingham Street garage to whom it has been loaned from Battersea for route 137. Although Victoria lost their scheduled RTLs upon the removal of an allocation for route 10 at the end of 1966, at this period a couple were retained there as RM spares for the 52 and 137. By now, Battersea's RTLs were being gradually replaced by RTs, resulting in this one's transfer to West Ham a few days later. It too then remained there until it perished on 7 September 1968 and went for scrap in November 1969.

**On 1/4/67**, RTL1235 stands outside the offices of its home garage, Stockwell. Withdrawn a few weeks later upon route 2's conversion to RM operation, this RTL remained in store for two years before going for scrap in April 1969.

**On the** same day, RTL77 heads south along Battersea Bridge Road on route 19 not far from its home garage. It will soon be transferred to Clapton as a result of RTs arriving at Battersea, and was withdrawn there in the autumn. It was sold to Ceylon in April 1968.

**In Battersea** garage itself, scenes like this will soon be a thing of the past as RTs are now replacing their RTLs. Of these two, RTL360 (on the left) moved to West Ham a few days later, where it remained until its inevitable withdrawal on 7 September 1968, and then went for scrap in May 1969, whilst RTL1291 (right) was withdrawn outright shortly afterwards and sold to Ceylon in December 1967.

**On 19/4/67**, Hackney RTL1146 heads east along Bloomsbury Way on route 22 shortly before withdrawal. Battersea's RTLs were now being replaced by RTs on this route, but Hackney's soldiered on until October, when RMs replaced them. This one was sold to Ceylon in July 1968.

**Seen down** the 'Dilly the same day, Stockwell RTL1043 stands in for an RM on route 88. Withdrawn shortly after this picture was taken, for some reason it spent two years in store at Sutton garage before going for scrap in June 1969.

**Also on** 19/4/67, Clapton RTL1131 speeds along Burdett Road, Limehouse on its long journey from Finsbury Park station to Becontree, Chitty's Lane. This RTL was also sold a few days after this picture was taken, but was sold to an independent operator in Ayrshire in July 1967 and saw some six years' service there before scrapping.

**Not far** away, Poplar roofbox RTL1438 has just changed crew at the northern approach to Blackwall Tunnel, as a new block of flats is being built for the Greater London Council to replace Victorian terrace houses that had survived the 1940/41 Blitz in this area. Withdrawn in common with all other surviving East End RTLs on 'Black Saturday', 7 September 1968, this one was dumped in its own garage until going for scrap in May 1969.

**For many** years, Poplar garage was used as a dump for withdrawn vehicles, which often outnumbered its working allocation! Two rows of them are seen here on the left-hand side of the garage, and Metro-Cammell-bodied RTL817 nearest the camera had been based there prior to withdrawal in the summer of 1966. It was sold to Ceylon in December 1967. RT3893 on the right, however, is merely delicensed awaiting Aldenham overhaul (which it had in July) and would survive at London's service until August 1975, and then see a further four years' use as a trainer.

**With its** lights already switched on for the run through Rotherhithe Tunnel, Poplar RTL1293 leaves Stepney East station on the same day. RTLs working this route, and the 108 and the 108A, had reinforced tyres to counteract their rubbing against the kerbs in the Blackwall and Rotherhithe tunnels. The RTs that replaced them on 7 September 1968 also had these, only for the 82 to be withdrawn and the 108 converted to MB operation on the following 26 October. Meanwhile, RTL1293 was withdrawn soon after this picture was taken, and sold to Ceylon in April 1968. The bridge behind it carries the former London & Blackwall Railway, by this time little used, due to the nearby docks now in terminal decline. It was resurrected in 1987 for the new Docklands Light Railway.

**On my** journey home that day, I encountered Clapton's RTL1335 at Old Street station working route 253A. It is followed by a roofbox RTL from the same garage on route 170, which paralleled the 253A from Bloomsbury to Clapton, Kenninghall Road roundabout. For some strange reason, RTL1335 had been on a trip to Prague, Czechoslovakia in 1965, yet was returned to service. Withdrawn in the spring of 1967 and then sold to Barton of Chilwell (via P.V.S.) in December 1967. It ran with them until November 1970, when it went for scrap.

**Although many** Metro-Cammell-bodied RTLs were exported to Ceylon, some found new homes with British independent operators. An example of this is former RTL659, which was sold to Wimbledon Coaches in September 1965 and saw some five years use with them. Here, it arrives at Wembley Stadium brining spectators to see the FA amateur cup final between Enfield and Skelmersdale United on 22/4/67.

**A visit** to Cricklewood garage on the same day finds RTL359 dumped at the back of the garage along with a batch of withdrawn Metro-Cammell-bodied RTLs. It had been there since late 1965, and finally went for scrap in September 1967. Note how its fleet name has been painted out.

**Inside the** garage, roofbox RTL1328 has been working route 240, which was shared with Edgware RTs. This RTL was withdrawn in March 1968, but then reinstated and sent to Bow, where it remained until withdrawal on that fateful day, 7 September 1968 and finally went for scrap in May 1969. Another withdrawn Metro-Cammell-bodied RTL stands behind it.

**RTL1564 has** just passed its home garage, Cricklewood which is on the left behind the railway bridge which carries the southern arm of the Dudden Hill loop to join the Midland main line. Route 142 was also shared with Edgware, and took RTLs out into the Country Area at Watford Junction, the last route to operate the type beyond the Central Area. This RTL was withdrawn shortly after this picture was taken, and was another to go to Ceylon in April 1968.

On 27/4/67, Clapton RTL1238 calls at County Hall, still my place of employment, on its way to Wandsworth on tram and trolleybus replacement route 170. This RTL was also withdrawn shortly after this picture was taken, and was another to be sold via P.V.S to Barton in December 1967. It remained with them until October 1970, going for scrap three months later, whilst those at Clapton in general were replaced by RTs in the autumn of 1967. Of note in this picture is the lion which has recently been placed on a pedestal overlooking the Thames. Unusually made of Portland stone, this had originally adorned the Lion Brewery on the South Bank, then after the war stood outside Waterloo station until bomb damage was reinstated along York Road. When I started 'work' at County Hall in January 1965, it was gathering dust in the building's basement, but two years later the Greater London Council wisely erected it outside County Hall, where it remains to this day.

Battersea RTL22 has just five days left in service when seen in Parliament Street bound for Southfields on route 39 on 24/4/67. For several years the lowest-numbered RTL in the fleet, this one was one of those overhauled to replace trolleybuses at Clapton depot in April 1959, then overhauled again in January 1963. It was sold to Ceylon in October 1967.

**A busy** scene in Kingsway the same day finds Stockwell RTL1400 heading south on the weekday 77A. This RTL was transferred to Cricklewood soon afterwards and withdrawn in November 1967. After that, it was dumped at Stonebridge Park and cannibalised for Ceylon, its remains being sold for scrap in April 1969. Of note is the building on the right, Africa House which had until recently housed a colonial high commission. As a notice visible beneath the RTLs canopy proclaims, it is now 'to be let'. It became J.D. Wetherspoons' pub 'The Shakespeare's Head' in the early 1990s, as it still is at the time of writing.

**Although route** 40 had converted to RM operation in the autumn of 1964, RTLs from both Poplar and West Ham garages still put in appearances on it until the end. In the evening rush hour of Thursday, 27/4/67, Poplar RTL547, one of those overhauled in late 1965, is seen at Gardiner's Corner with a short working to Aldgate from the east. This RTL was withdrawn with scores of others on 7 September 1968, remaining in store until April 1969. However, this one was a survivor, being exported to Australia where it is preserved!

**This chance** shot shows RTL414 on its way from Battersea, where it has just been replaced by RTs, passing through Aldgate to reallocation in the east, in this case at West Ham. RTLs such as this one, which had been overhauled more recently (this one was done in October 1964) were moved on to replace others that had been done earlier. RTL414 perished on 'Black Saturday', 7 September 1968 and eventually went for scrap in November 1969. Note the wartime bomb damage behind the RTL, only now being reinstated 26 years after the Blitz.

**New tower** blocks rise in the City in the background of this view of Poplar roofbox RTL1438, which we saw earlier on route 108, as it sets off from Aldgate for Blackwall Tunnel on a scheduled rush hour RTL-operated journey of the 23, which had otherwise been RM-operated since the spring of 1964. At this time, Aldgate High Street still had two-way traffic.

**A rare** working later on the evening of 27/4/67 is that of Bow RTL1315 seen crossing the Great Eastern main line at Norton Folgate while covering for an RM on route 8A, which had converted from RTW to RM early in 1965. This RTL was withdrawn in the summer of 1967, and sold to P.V.S. (dealers) in September. It was exported to Canada where it later ran on tours around the Niagara Falls, ending up as a mobile chip bar.

**About to** turn from Shoreditch High Street into Great Eastern Street on the same evening, Clapton RTL540 has only a few days left in service. Although route 170 usually ran all the way from Leyton to Wandsworth, it had many short journeys that terminated from the east at Bloomsbury, or as in this case, Clerkenwell Green. These had previously been worked by trolleybus route 555, which tram replacement route 170 had been extended to replace in April 1959. RTL540 was sold to Ceylon in April 1968.

On 28/4/67, RTL1319 runs out from Battersea garage across Battersea Bridge for the evening rush hour. It is not evident whether the No.22 following, which is also running out from the garage, is an RT or an RTL – the latter were now rapidly being swept away. As for RTL1319, it was transferred to Cricklewood, but withdrawn in November and then sold to Ceylon in July 1968.

On 30/4/67, RTL22, which we saw earlier on route 39, has just been withdrawn and is one of several about to be driven away from Battersea garage following replacement by RTs and placed into store at Camberwell garage. For several years the lowest-numbered RTL in the fleet, this one was one of those overhauled to replace trolleybuses at Clapton depot in April 1959, then overhauled again in January 1963. It was sold to Ceylon in October 1967.

**At Victoria** the same evening, Stockwell RTL1294 on the Vauxhall Bridge Road stand of the 2 is about to be overtaken by RM162 on route 2B, which had received RMs in October 1966. It would be the 2 and 2A's turn in June, when this RTL was transferred to Cricklewood, where it would be withdrawn in September. It too went to Ceylon, in April 1968.

**RTL1321, another** from Stockwell, stands in for an RM on route 88 in Parliament Street on 2/5/67. It was now the turn of this garage to lose its RTLs, now the last based in South London. Originally planned as a trolleybus depot, the huge Stockwell bus garage opened in 1951 with a large allocation of RTLs to replace local trams. This RTL was transferred to Hackney where it was withdrawn on 7 September 1968. It went for scrap in May 1969.

**Although P.V.S.** sold many ex-London Transport vehicles on to various operators, this one, former RTL867, which they had bought in August 1966 after a private individual had bought it and taken it on a holiday to Spain (hence the slipboard just visible), passed to their associated fleets Super Coaches and City Coaches of Upminster, who operated it for some three years before it went for scrap in 1970. This view finds it on an Omnibus Touring Circle trip to the Brighton HCVC Rally on 7/5/67, stopping somewhere en route for a refreshment break. This Metro-Cammell-bodied RTL had been withdrawn when replaced by RTs at Walworth garage in the spring of 1966.

**One of** the first RTLs to be preserved was RTL1323. Originally sold for use as a furniture showroom in August 1964, it went into preservation two years later. It was absurdly adorned in Green Line livery, as seen here also at the 1967 Brighton HCVC event – no RTL ever carried Green Line livery in reality, and this one was not even one of the eighteen RTLs overhauled in green Country Area livery in 1959! The vehicle remained in this silly livery for many years and, on this occasion, its owners could not even give it a correct blind display! It still exists today, thankfully restored in its correct red livery.

**At the** same event, RTW467 is also preserved, but this time in its correct livery, except for its fleet name which, at this period, was obliged to be removed since London Transport frowned upon privately owned buses carrying it. It had been the last RTW in service (at Brixton garage) a year previously and is still going strong today.

**At this** period, I had the pleasure of travelling to and from 'work' at County Hall by route 171 from Essex Road. The route was now shared by Walworth RTs and Tottenham RTLs, of which RTL294 is seen passing County Hall on 9/5/67. This one was withdrawn in September 1967 and sold to Ceylon in August 1968. Of note here are the Greater London Council's works (supervised by the office in which I was based) to build a roundabout at the junction of Westminster Bridge Road, York Road and Addington Street. Shortly after it was completed, the Council built its monstrous County Hall Island Block on the site. Fortunately, this was demolished a few years ago and a hotel stands there now!

**On the** same occasion, Stockwell RTL1436 on route 77A has for some reason been diverted over Westminster Bridge instead of running along Millbank and over Lambeth Bridge, taking the routeing of the weekend 77C. This RTL moved to Poplar after displacement by RTs, but was withdrawn in October 1967 and sold in May 1968 to a private owner for conversion to a caravan for an overseas holiday. Note on the left the old St. Thomas's Hospital, which was badly damaged by wartime bombing and demolished in 1968.

**For several** years, Willesden garage had a Saturday allocation on otherwise RM-operated route 18. At first using RTWs, this changed to RTL in the spring of 1965 and lasted until 'Black Saturday', 7 September 1968. On 13/5/67, an almost empty RTL1506 heads for London Bridge along Wembley High Road. Withdrawn shortly after this picture was taken, it was sold to Ceylon in April 1968.

**Next day**, early in the morning of 14/5/67, Stockwell RTL1435 is seen at Trafalgar Square working their small Sunday allocation of weekend route 77B. This one was withdrawn as a result of the influx of RMs and RTs to Stockwell during the summer of 1967, and exported to Holland where it was preserved in April 1968.

**A familiar** sight around Waterloo and Westminster at this time was former RTL1256, owned by Albert Harling Coaches of Lambeth and used for nurses' transport to and from hospitals in the area. This was one of the eighteen RTLs overhauled in green livery for the Country Area in 1959 and latterly used for driver training. It was deroofed in the summer of 1962 in a low bridge accident, and sold in September that year to Harling's, who fitted a roof to it from a scrapped RT! This view sees it in York Road, Waterloo on 17/5/67. Today, it is smartly preserved in 1959 London Transport Country Area livery. Here, its non-standard front offside hub-cap produces an odd effect!

**Immediately before** withdrawal, Poplar RTL1158 stands at a temporary terminus for routes 108 and 108A in Devas Street, Bromley-By-Bow, as a result of GLC road works associated with the new Bow Bridge flyover on 22/5/67. It was sold to Ceylon in December 1967. The RF behind it is on a railway emergency service for the District Line, which was also disrupted by these works at nearby Bromley-By-Bow station.

**In Poplar** garage itself that day, RTL1183 and RTL1192 are in store on the right-hand side of the garage in addition to three rows of withdrawn RTLs and RTWs on its left! Both had been withdrawn from Clapton garage earlier in the year. RTL1183 was sold to a firm in Strood, Kent for use as a staff bus in November, whilst RTL1192 went to an independent operator in Ayrshire who kept it in service for a further seven years.

**Also in** the garage, standing next to the two withdrawn RTLs seen above, RTL424 bears the special blind for the PLA dockers' service. It would perish on 'Black Saturday', 7 September 1968, and go for scrap in June 1969.

**A number** of routes terminated at Blackwall Tunnel and here, also on 22/5/67, Poplar RTL75 is on one of the many short workings of route 106 that terminated there, accompanying an RT on the western section of the long route 175. For the benefit of crews working to this terminus, there was a London Transport canteen in nearby East India Dock Road, which had also replaced facilities at Athol Street garage when it closed in 1960. RTL75 was amongst the hundreds of RTLs which perished on 'Black Saturday', 7 September 1968, and finally went for scrap in November 1969.

**A real** oddity in the RTL fleet was RTL626, which had been overhauled by mistake with a standard Park Royal body in January 1962, instead of a Metro-Cammell one. It was, moreover, one of the 100 RTLs given another overhaul in the latter part of 1965 and ended up surviving in service to the very end of RTL operation. That is in the future, though, when it is seen working from Clapton garage in Mare Street, Hackney on 25/5/67 on route 253A. RTL626 also survived after withdrawal by being sold to a private preservationist in Belgium in May 1969.

**7/6/67 was** the last day that RTLs operated from Battersea garage, and here on that final day, RTL1459 heads along Battersea Bridge Road on route 39's evening rush hour extension to Tottenham garage. It incorrectly shows the via blind for the Saturday working which only ventured as far north as Victoria. This RTL was one of the last to be overhauled in their normal overhaul cycle (in February 1965) prior to which it had always retained its original body having been on an overseas tour promoting Britain when new. Next day, it was transferred to Poplar garage, but unfortunately was involved in a serious rear-end collision in Blackwall Tunnel in September and written off for scrap and dumped at Stonebridge Park, from where its remains were sold in April 1969.

**Route 19** is one that I have known since early childhood, when RTLs working it from Battersea garage were new. Now, 7/6/67, it is their last day doing so and here is RTL1577 seen in trendy Kings Road, Chelsea. Overhauled only once, in March 1962, with Weymann body No.9160 which was new to RTL1590 and did not enter service until the spring of 1958, it was withdrawn next day and sold, via P.V.S., to Barton of Chilwell in December 1967, working for them until withdrawal in March 1972. Behind it follows Hackney RTL1146 on the 22. This was withdrawn a few weeks later and sold to Ceylon in July 1968.

**Another RTW** to see use with a British independent operator was RTW367, sold to Roydonian Coaches, based near Harlow, Essex, in March 1967. They kept it for six years, before breaking it up for scrap. This view finds it in Victoria Street on 7/6/67 in their maroon and cream livery.

**Although route** 16 had been one of the first to convert from RT-types to RM operation, in December 1962, RTLs from Cricklewood garage often strayed onto it until their demise at the garage in October 1968. Thus, also on 7/6/67, their RTL1269 is seen at Victoria Station. Withdrawn a few weeks after this picture was taken, it did not go for scrap until January 1970.

**At the** premises of Staffordshire independent operator Harper Brothers of Heath Hayes, the body of RTW110 is dumped on its side when seen on 18/6/67. This had been sold in March 1965 and was used for a year or so by a Midlands beat group as a touring vehicle, before being acquired by Harper's for spare parts eighteen months later.

**Former RTL26** was no doubt one of Harper's vehicles to benefit from the cannibalisation of RTW110! This was one of the early RTL sales, acquired by Harper's via the dealer Bird's of Stratford-upon-Avon in August 1958. When Midland Red took over Harper's in September 1974, RTL26 became their No.2201, though it was never operated by them and sold for scrap soon afterwards.

**Dumped outside** Cricklewood garage on 11/7/67, Metro-Cammell-bodied RTLs 657, 997 and 947 make a sad sight. All three, however, saw further use in Ceylon, RTL947 going in July 1968 and the other two in December that year.

**Passing its** home garage, Clapton, on 20/8/67, RTL442 works Sunday-only route 106A. From 1 September, RTs will start to replace RTLs at this garage, which hitherto had had a 100% allocation of RTLs since its conversion from a trolleybus depot in April 1959. It was the last garage to be all-RTL. This RTL was transferred in November to Cricklewood, where it was withdrawn along with route 60 on 'Black Saturday', 7 September 1968. It went for scrap in June 1969 after cannibalisation for spares for Ceylon at Stonebridge Park.

**West Ham's** large allocation of RTLs for route 25 often substituted for RMs on trolleybus replacement routes at the garage. On 29/9/67, RTL414 which we saw earlier on transfer to West Ham, stands at a very wet and dismal Stratford Broadway on route 69.

**In the** morning rush hour of Monday, 9/10/67, Tottenham roofbox RTL1456 is stuck in traffic at The Angel, Islington and very unusually curtailed to Brockley Rise. This was my bus to 'work' at County Hall that morning. Withdrawn when RTs replaced Tottenham's RTLs on route 171 in June 1968, it went for scrap in May 1969.

**By 21/10/67**, the furthest from Central London that RTLs reached in service was Watford Junction, to where we see Cricklewood RTL1552 on route 142 heading north through Bushey. Just over a year later, RTs replaced RTLs at this garage, when this one was withdrawn. It went for scrap in November 1969.

**Also in** Bushey that day, we find ex-RTL362 which had been sold by LT in August 1959. At this period it was operated by Knightswood Coaches of Watford, by whom it was withdrawn in April 1969.

**By 9** November 1967, all London Transport's RT-type driver trainer buses were RTWs. Typical of them is RTW58, seen at Islington Green. Retired in December 1969, it went for scrap in March 1971.

**All except** a handful of 3RT3s based in the Country Area of London Transport's double-deck staff buses were RTLs at this period too. Seen within the confines of Aldenham Works on this same day is RTL438. In common with most of the fleet it had been demoted to staff bus duties in 1960 (replacing 2RT2s) and recently been repainted. However despite its smart appearance here, it was retired in December 1967 and then cannibalised for spare parts for Ceylon before going for scrap in April 1969.

**RTL70 was** seriously damaged in a collision when working from Stockwell garage in 1965. Its remains were taken to Aldenham and cannibalised for spare parts. This was all that was left of it there on 9/11/67. It went for scrap the following month.

**RTLs that** were reconditioned prior to sale (usually to Ceylon) were sent to various garages around the fleet (including the Country Area) where LT mechanics often worked on them on overtime. Such was the case on 11/11/67 with RTL720 and RTL329 in Sutton garage. These two, however, did not go to Ceylon: RTL329 was exported to the USA in July 1968, whilst RTL720 ended up going for scrap in June 1969.

**Seen at** Becontree Heath bus station on 18/11/67, RTL140 has just been transferred from Clapton to Bow garage, to where it is about to run in on route 25. It remained there until 'Black Saturday', 7 September 1968 and went for scrap in May 1969. Of note in this picture is the LT canteen and the two timekeeping clocks on its wall on the right. This was the furthest east that RTLs now reached in service.

**Haven Green**, Ealing was now the furthest point west RTLs reached, on route 112 which was jointly worked with Palmers Green RTs. On 19/11/67, Stonebridge Park RTL1041 waits there before its long journey around the North Circular Road. It was withdrawn in September 1968 and dismantled for spares for Ceylon at its own garage before going for scrap in June 1969.

**Roofbox RTL1475** was one of the last to operate from Clapton garage when seen crossing Westminster Bridge on route 170 on 22/11/67. It was transferred to Tottenham garage a couple of days after this picture was taken, withdrawn from there in June 1968 and sold for scrap in May 1969.

**On a** snowy Saturday, 9/12/67, former RTL1004 is seen in Streatham High Road in use as a mobile road safety exhibition for Lambeth Council, to whom it had been sold in June 1967. Later exported to Guernsey for sightseeing use and rebuilt with a forward entrance and central staircase, it has since returned to mainland Britain and been preserved.

**Snow is** still evident later the same day as Poplar RTL375 approaches Eltham, Well Hall station on its way to Bromley-by-Bow on tunnel route 108A. Eltham was now the furthest south that surviving RTLs reached. This one was yet another that perished on 'Black Saturday', 7/9/68, and then remained in store at Poplar until going for scrap in May 1969.

**For several** years, Tottenham garage had a Saturday allocation on route 191, which ran from Enfield Town to Chingford Hatch. On 16/12/67, their roofbox RTL144 approaches the junction of the North Circular Road and Fore Street, Edmonton. This RTL had recently been withdrawn at Dalston garage but reinstated at Tottenham, where it remained until ousted by RTs on route 171 in June 1968; it too went for scrap in May 1969.

**Seen next** day, 17/12/67 passing the Lewisham Theatre at Rushey Green, Poplar RTL1582 works tunnel route 108 through to Crystal Palace, which it only did at weekends at this period, otherwise terminating at Lower Sydenham. This RTL also perished on 7 September 1968, remaining in store at Poplar until going for scrap in January 1970.

**A very** unusual occurrence on 19/12/67 was the appearance of Hackney RTL1321 on route 6, which by now was RML-operated. It escorts an RM and an RML along Fleet Street and made me late for 'work' that morning! Running back to its home garage, it remained there until the fateful 7 September 1968, and also went for scrap in May 1969.

**Seen on** 30/12/67 in heavy traffic due to a home match at nearby Arsenal Stadium, Hackney RTL1308 turns from Brownswood Road into Blackstock Road, Finsbury Park on route 106. On match days, extra buses were borrowed from Dalston garage for this route. This RTL was yet another to perish on 7 September 1968, but did not go for scrap until February 1970.

**As 1968** dawned, the main concentrations of surviving RTLs were at Hackney, Bow, Poplar and West Ham garages in the east, and Cricklewood, Stonebridge Park and Willesden in the north-west of London. Otherwise there were just two small allocations at Dalston (for the 47 and 78) and Tottenham for the 171. On the latter, RTL1597 pulls away from the stop outside County Hall in York Road, Waterloo from where I used to catch the 171 home from work. RTLs at Tottenham had begun to be replaced by RTs in December 1967, but owing to an increase in RT overhauls in January, these were removed and the RTLs reinstated. They were replaced at both Dalston and Tottenham in June 1968. This one survived to work another three months at West Ham prior to its inevitable withdrawal on 7/9/68. It went for scrap in December 1969.

The well-known school contract and private hire company run by the Margolis family had become known as The South London Coach Company by the time their Metro-Cammell-bodied former RTL901 was seen in Victoria on 19/1/68. It still looks in good condition, despite a dent on its nearside front dome, and was sold to Margo's (as the company was colloquially known) in August 1966, and withdrawn by them just over five years later.

On Sunday, 6/1/68, RTL459 heads a group of its fellows outside West Ham garage. Exactly eight months later, all RTLs in the east would be withdrawn and in fact many had a stay of execution, owing to the busmen's union being unhappy with the terms under which new one-man-operated MB-types would work. This RTL was one of the very last to be overhauled (in January 1966) but was still withdrawn on 7/9/68 and went for scrap in December 1969. Their withdrawal during the year was therefore foreseen at this time, but the closure of the large West Ham garage by the Tory LRT regime in October 1992 was certainly not!

On a very cold, grey Monday morning, 22/1/68, Tottenham roofbox RTL144 has taken me to 'work' at County Hall on one of the rush hour short workings the 171 ran there from Rosebery Avenue. These were intended to take commuters from Waterloo station to the Holborn area; thus I had a virtually empty bus to myself travelling in the opposite direction. This particular RTL, although it had its windows locked shut for the winter, was like an ice-box, since some of them did not fit properly, as a close look at it will reveal! Withdrawn in June, it went for scrap in May 1969. The crowds of commuters seen in this picture are waiting for buses on routes such as the 46, 70, 76 or 149 to take them to the Millbank, Westminster and Victoria areas. New 'Red Arrow' routes 503 and 507 would be introduced to replace all but the 149 on 7 September.

On 27/1/68, Dalston RTL505 passes the closed North London Line station at Shoreditch, at the time used by dressmaking firm Alfred Goldberg. It is bound for Stamford Hill, to where the 47 had been extended already in July 1961 in conjunction with trolleybus replacement. This RTL was transferred to West Ham in June when Dalston lost RTLs, but withdrawn on 'Black Saturday', 7 September, also going for scrap in May 1969.

**Another RTL** on route 47 took me to Surrey Docks station, where Poplar RTL384 is seen on Rotherhithe Tunnel route 82. Ironically, today, London Overground services link Dalston, Shoreditch and Surrey Docks, now renamed Surrey Quays. Meanwhile, this roofbox RTL also perished on 7 September 1968, and went for scrap in May 1969.

**Further south** on the same day, Poplar RTL1499 climbs through Lower Sydenham towards Crystal Palace on Blackwall Tunnel route 108. This too perished on 'Black Saturday' despite being another of the last RTLs overhauled, only in January 1966, but did not go for scrap until February 1970.

**On a** wet Sunday, 4/2/68, staff bus RTL310 stands outside Walthamstow garage and is officially attached to nearby Leyton to take staff to and from Aldenham and Chiswick Works. Of note is the Ford Thames Trader lorry in the background, one of many in London Transport's service vehicle fleet at the time. RTL310 was retired in February 1969 and went for scrap the following May.

**Willesden RTL1526** has a good load aboard when seen heading for Edgware on route 18 at Paddington Green on 10/2/68. This RTL lasted at Willesden until the very end (30/11/68), being cannibalised for spares for Ceylon before going for scrap in January 1970.

**On 13/2/68**, a friend phoned me at 'work' to tell me that Tottenham roofbox RTL1475 was working route 76 in place of one of their troublesome Leyland Atlanteans. My office was at the other end of the large County Hall complex to Westminster Bridge, but this did not stop me from 'escaping' to catch it passing the building, in typically foul February weather!

**This view** of a well-laden Cricklewood roofbox RTL1328 bound for Watford on route 142 on 17/2/68 shows it passing Duple's coachbuilding factory at West Hendon. A string of trolleybus traction standards are still in use as street lighting columns. RTL1328 was withdrawn in March, but reinstated at the beginning of April at Bow garage, where it remained until 'Black Saturday', 7/9/68, when it finally perished. It went for scrap in May 1969.

**Dalston RTLs** still put in appearances on route 11 covering for RMs until the end. On 5/3/68, their RTL1610 passes Westminster City Hall in Victoria Street. This RTL was another that survived RT replacement in June, moving to West Ham until 'Black Saturday', 7/9/68. It went for scrap in November 1969.

**On 10/3/68**, Willesden RTL1338 is seen near 'The Prince of Wales' in Harrow Road, North Kensington to where it has been curtailed on their Saturday allocation of route 18, and already has its blinds set for return to Sudbury. Peculiarly, although Stonebridge Park operated a major share of this route and also had a small allocation of RTLs for the 112, they seldom if ever strayed on to the 18. This RTL was another to stay at Willesden until the very end, also being cannibalised for spares for Ceylon and finally sent for scrap in December 1969.

**A derailment** at, of all places, St. James's Park on the Circle and District Lines in the evening rush hour of 4/4/68 necessitated a major railway emergency bus service between Charing Cross and Victoria stations. This view shows Poplar RTL1582 performing this at Parliament Square in already heavy traffic. This RTL joined the hundreds of its fellows withdrawn on 7 September 1968 and was sold in January 1970, ostensibly for possible further use, to Bird's of Stratford-upon-Avon.

**A bizarre** sight in Hertford garage on 6/4/68 is that of RTL1028 which had been sold to Ceylon in December 1967 but dropped from the crane when it was being loaded at the docks, with the result seen here! The unfortunate RTL was returned to London Transport and cannibalised for spares for Ceylon, and eventually went for scrap in April 1969. In this view, it accompanies GS13, which is now preserved.

**At Harlow** garage the same day, trainer RTW271 has a rest for the weekend. This was the last new London Transport Country Area garage built, opened in 1963, and is one of few to survive in use at the time of writing. The array of LT 'dolly stops' in the background is interesting! RTW271 was retired in February 1970 and sold for scrap in April 1971.

**A big** surprise at this time was the appearance of roofbox RTL1328 at Bow garage, after its withdrawal from service at Cricklewood in March. It is seen here on 8/4/68 outside the Army and Navy Stores in Victoria Street. It was withdrawn on 7/9/68, as mentioned previously.

**RTLs from** Poplar garage still covered for RMs on route 40A until the end. On 11/4/68, their RTL1585 heads north at Elephant & Castle in the evening rush hour. One of the last to be overhauled, in January 1966, it was nevertheless withdrawn on 'Black Saturday' 7/9/68, remaining in store at Poplar until going for scrap in February 1970.

**On Easter** Monday, 21/4/68, the odd RTL626 sets off from Golders Green station working route 226 from Willesden garage, where it would remain until the very end, on 30 November 1968.

**Despite its** conversion to RM operation in the autumn of 1966, route 52 still had visits from Willesden RTLs until the end. RTL1513 calls at Hyde Park Corner on a short working from Victoria to Ladbroke Grove in the evening rush hour of 25/4/68. This one also lasted until the end and went for scrap in October 1969.

**As mentioned** earlier, the famous independent Nottinghamshire operator, Barton of Chilwell, owned several RTLs. Former RTL1335, which we saw earlier working from Clapton garage, is seen with some of its fellows in their Ilkeston depot on 28/4/68. It had been sold to them (via P.V.S.) in December 1967 and remained in use until November 1970.

**For some** reason, Barton also had one solitary RTW, former RTW341, seen also at Ilkeston. Their red, cream and brown livery suited the ex-London vehicles. Acquired in December 1965, it was withdrawn by Barton in September 1971.

**Time is** now running out for all RTLs remaining in service, including Poplar roofbox RTL384, seen at Eltham Church on tunnel route 108A on 2/5/68. It would perish just four months later on 7/9/68, and went for scrap in May 1969.

**THE place** to be to observe surviving RTWs in 1968 was Chiswick High Road on weekdays, where many could be seen running to and from Chiswick Works on training duties. Here on 9/5/68, RTW495, one of those attached to the Country Area, is about to arrive there. Quite why the cafe on the right should be called 'Depot Dining Rooms' is a mystery to me, considering that there was a splendid staff canteen within the works! This RTW was retired from use at Hertford in September 1969 and sold for scrap two months later.

**On the** same day, RTW389, another one based in the Country Area, dwarfs lowbridge RLH24 in the yard of Addlestone garage. This RTW was retired in December 1969 and sold for scrap in August 1970.

**A month** before Dalston lost their RTLs, RTL1574 heads north along Norton Folgate to route 78's nearby Shoreditch terminus on 14/5/68. It was another to move to West Ham for almost three months prior to withdrawal on 'Black Saturday', going for scrap in June 1969.

**The 78** shared its Shoreditch Church terminal stand with route 47, on which Dalston roofbox RTL1427 has arrived the same day. Withdrawn a month later, this RTL was sold initially to P.V.S. in May 1969, moving on to work as a staff bus for various companies, before being secured for preservation late in 1977.

**Not often** seen was this 'lazy' blind display for short journeys on routes 108 and 108A between Blackwall Tunnel north and Bromley-by-Bow, intended for use when the tunnel was closed. RTL494 is seen just north of the tunnel on 17/5/68. Withdrawn on 'Black Saturday', 7/9/68, it was another sold to Bird's for possible re-use in January 1970.

**Seen bouncing** over Stratford Broadway's famous cobblestones also on 17/5/68, RTL1337 was an oddity. Its original body and registration number (MXX40) were for some reason given to RT4668 in 1952, and it did not appear until late 1954 thus explaining the 'OLD' registration. By now, however, that was irrelevant: based at Bow garage it was withdrawn with all the others on 'Black Saturday', 7 September 1968 and sold (to Bird's) in December 1969.

**At Super** Coaches/Upminster & District's depot on 18/5/68, former RTL811 is being broken up for spares. It had been sold to a group of 'trendy lefty' students at the West Kent College for Further Education for a trip to the USSR in January 1967, and was acquired by Super in December that year. Does anyone know if it actually reached Leningrad?

**The last** time an RTL ever operated from a South London garage was on Derby Day, 29/5/68, when Cricklewood RTL418 was loaned to Putney, Chelverton Road to work extra journeys on route 93. Here it has arrived at Epsom Market Place much to the apparent amusement of the point inspector seen talking to its driver! RTLs had worked at this garage on the 93 until replaced by RTs in the autumn of 1965. This one was withdrawn along with route 60 on 'Black Saturday' and went for scrap in June 1969 after being stripped for spare parts at Stonebridge Park for Ceylon.

**On route** 60 itself, roofbox RTL453 arrives at Waterloo on 30/5/68. Destined to be the last roofbox RTL in service when withdrawn from Cricklewood garage at the end of October 1968, it was rescued for preservation in February 1970 and forms part of the Ensignbus heritage fleet today.

**On the** evening of 14/6/68, RTL337 makes its very last run in public service, on the short trip from Bruce Grove station, where it is seen, to Tottenham garage. RTs will replace the RTLs here on the 171 next day. This RTL went for scrap in May 1969.

**Its blinds** removed for re-use in an RT, roofbox RTL144 leaves Tottenham garage for the last time, to go into store, first at Peckham and then at Bexleyheath garage before also going for scrap in May 1969. No more would I enjoy a ride to and from 'work' at County Hall on one of these vehicles!

**Seen at** the Jubilee Clock, Harlesden, Willesden RTL1440 works a rush hour journey to Park Royal Stadium, adjacent to the factory where over 65% of RTL bodies were built, on 5/7/68. This was another to last until the end and then be cannibalised for spare parts for Ceylon at Stonebridge Park prior to sale for scrap in June 1969.

**For some** reason, nearly all of West Ham's Saturday allocation on route 40, which should have been RM-operated, was worked by RTLs on 6/7/68, altering the course of a 'Red Rover' jaunt I was doing that day when I encountered them at London Bridge; instead of heading south to Eltham, I headed east on one of them! Here at Plaistow, Greengate, West Ham roofbox RTL409 runs into the garage after a trip to Wanstead station and back. Withdrawn on 'Black Saturday' two months later, this RTL was another to make the one-way trip to the Yorkshire scrapyards in May 1969.

**Seen at** Blackheath, Royal Standard on 15/7/68, Poplar RTL1528 works to the 108's weekday terminus of Lower Sydenham, Bell Green. This RTL shared the same fate as the one seen above.

**An oddity** for many years on route 25 was its short journeys during rush hours between Dagenham, Ford's and Dagenham East Station, where West Ham RTL414 stands on 18/7/68. These journeys were not connected with the main 25 route which ran from Becontree Heath to Victoria, other than when running in or out of West Ham garage, and by now were little used, since for obvious reasons most Ford's workers drove to and from work! Also withdrawn on 7/9/78, this RTL went for scrap in November 1969.

**The last** route to take RTLs through semi-rural territory was the 240 between Golders Green and Edgware, with whose RTs Cricklewood garage shared it. Here on 19/7/68, their subsequently famous roofbox RTL453 is seen at Mill Hill East station.

**On the** same day, New Cross staff bus RTL394 leaves Aldenham Works bound for home. For many years, this had been fitted with additional rainstrips above its front upper deck windows, to keep out draughts, giving it this odd appearance! Retired from staff bus duties in November 1969, it went for scrap the following month.

**Although Clapton's** main allocation of RTLs on route 277 had been withdrawn by the end of 1967, Poplar garage had a small share on it at weekends which carried on until 'Black Saturday', 7/9/68. Their RTL1418 is seen passing Hackney Central Hall in Mare Street on 20/7/68, some seven weeks before the end.

**To illustrate** how withdrawn RTLs were farmed out to far-flung garages for reconditioning work, RTL110 and RTL559, the latter one of the last Metro-Cammell-bodied RTLs to be withdrawn in the summer of 1967, are seen in Stevenage Country Area garage on 28/7/68. RTL559 went next month to Ceylon, followed by RTL110 in December. Of note also is the Redshaw-Lister depot sweeper on the left, which was given a registration number (520UNK) since it had to travel across the public highway to also sweep the bus station!

**The end** is just four weeks away as Hackney RTL1601 is seen at Clapton Pond on route 106 on 10/8/68. This RTL was also an oddity, having been delivered earlier in 1954 than those in its sequence, and thereby not being stored until 1958 before entering service. It also originally had a Weymann body. Another of the last RTLs overhauled in January 1966, it too perished on 'Black Saturday', eventually going for scrap in November 1969.

**On 17/8/68**, the number of withdrawn RTLs stored in Poplar garage has grown, even though their own are still in service! Here, RTLs 315, 128 and 363 are nearest the camera. RTL315 was sold to a firm in Barking as a staff bus a few days after this picture was taken, and exported to Germany ten years later. Roofbox RTL128 was sold to a school in King's Lynn in September but scrapped two years later, whilst RTL363 languished in store until going for scrap in November 1969.

**Perhaps the** last really bizarre working of an RTL at London's service occurred on 21 August 1968, when West Ham RTL502 was used on the normally RML-operated route 249. Both the route and the RTL perished just over two weeks later on 'Black Saturday', 7 September 1968; the latter would also go for scrap in November 1969. Here, after coming up behind me and nearly giving me a heart attack at Chingford Green, RTL502 waits to reverse onto the 249's stand at the Royal Forest Hotel.

It is the last day of RTLs working in the East End, Friday, 6 September 1968, and Hackney RTL1601 and Poplar RTL1560 stand beneath the rusting girders of the uncompleted facade and extra platforms built for the Northern City Line's extension to Highgate and Alexandra Palace at Finsbury Park station on route 106. The former went for scrap in Yorkshire in November 1969, the latter to Bird's in January 1970.

At the start of the evening rush hour of their final day, West Ham RTL1607, one of those transferred from Dalston in June, heads a group of them on routes 10 and 25 in Aldgate bus station. By now, RTs are already taking their place on these routes. The streets of Aldgate and Whitechapel will no longer resound to the roar of their Leyland engines! This one will go for scrap in May 1969.

**Further to** the east, roofbox RTL384 stands at the Blackwall Tunnel terminus of route 56. Also on its last day of service, this had the oldest body (No.2129, originally new to RT850) still in use in the London Transport fleet at the time. It went for scrap in May 1969.

**Two weeks** after their withdrawal, so many RTLs were stored in Poplar garage that they were impeding the operation of their service buses. Therefore, on 21/9/68, several are being moved out for storage at Holloway and Finchley garages. This view shows RTL524 heading for the latter as two young bus spotters note the proceedings. All of the vehicles were on trade plates, as clearly shown here, since their licences were surrendered once they were no longer needed for service. This RTL went for scrap in February 1970.

**Meanwhile, groups** of dead RTLs and RTWs had accumulated at other garages. Here at Walthamstow on 29/9/68, RTL1237, RTL340, RTW482 and RTL1471 are dumped out the back of the garage. All went for scrap during 1969, the RTW having been cannibalised for spares for Ceylon at Stonebridge Park in the meantime.

**The only** surviving RTLs in service were now in north-west London at Willesden, Cricklewood and Stonebridge Park garages. RTL266 from the latter is seen at a very wet Haven Green, Ealing on Saturday, 19/10/68, unusually working short to Brent Station. Withdrawn with all those at Cricklewood and its own garage a week later on 26 October, it went for scrap in June 1969.

On 22/2/69, a group of dead RTLs await their fate in Clapton garage. They are headed by (left to right) RTL1604, 1588 and 164 which had come from nearby Hackney on 'Black Saturday', 7/9/68. The latter went for scrap in May 1969, the others in February 1970.

At Bexleyheath garage on 22/3/69, RTL289 and RTL428 are part of a line-up of withdrawn RTLs, many of which (as these two were) had been withdrawn from Tottenham garage in June 1968. They had previously been stored under cover in Peckham garage, which explains the pigeons' mess on RTL289's front dome! Both went for scrap in May 1969.

**At Stonebridge**
Park garage on 7/4/69, former Poplar RTL1459 is among a group of RTLs that have been cannibalised for spare parts. Its rear end damage is clearly visible and it went for scrap in May 1969.

**Also with** heavy rear-end damage at Stonebridge Park the same day, RTL1387 had been withdrawn as a result at Stockwell early in 1967. Metro-Cammell-bodied RTL684 and two RTWs complete the line-up. RTL1387 was cannibalised for Ceylon and went for scrap a few days after this picture was taken; RTL684 and the others went in May.

**Even more** badly damaged at Stonebridge Park that day is the unfortunate RTL1028, which had been dropped from the crane when embarking for Ceylon in December 1967. It has now been stripped of mechanical parts and went for scrap a few days later.

**On 3/5/69**, this line-up of withdrawn RTLs stand just how they were parked when they ran in to West Ham garage for the last time on 7 September 1968. RTL1607 and RTL96 are nearest the camera. All went for scrap shortly after this picture was taken.

**Some RTLs** were still running in the London area at this period. Here, on the same day, Metro-Cammell-bodied RTL758 is one of three used on school contracts by Walden's coaches of Epping. Bought in September 1966, it was however sold in the same month this shot was taken to another operator after replacement by a Saunders-bodied RT, and went for scrap in September 1969.

**Also still** active at this time was RTL1557, which had been acquired by a film company in June 1968. Seen at Highbury Corner on 6/6/69, it is on its way back to the film studios after featuring in the horror film Son of Jack the Ripper which was filmed the previous night in Whitechapel. Note the curious mixture of blinds and the cover over its fleet name.

**Caught on** my way to 'work' at Highbury Corner on 11/5/69, RTL1408 makes its final journey to the Yorkshire scrapyards from Poplar where it had been in store since withdrawal from Bow garage on 'Black Saturday', 7 September 1968.

**On 8/6/69**, this group of withdrawn RTLs make a sad sight in the rear (Stanley Road) yard of Fulwell garage. Nearest the camera is Metro-Cammell-bodied RTL907 which had been in store for almost three years. It finally went for scrap a few days after this picture was taken.

**Another Metro-** Cammell RTL to languish in store this late was RTL925, seen covered in dust in Bow garage on 14/6/69. It finally went for scrap in November that year.

**In their** last couple of years, many RTW training buses were smartened up, including having grey waistbands which they never carried in service. On 24/10/69, RTW104 is seen in Wembley. Retired in December, this one went for scrap in July 1970.

**The last** RTL staff bus to be used by London Transport was RTL1232. This view sees it leaving Chiswick Works for Abbey Wood on 26/5/70. It was finally withdrawn in October that year and sold for scrap in April 1971.

**A shortage** of RT training vehicles in the summer of 1978 caused London Transport to hire RT-types from preservationists. These included a few RTLs, the oddest of which was RTL525, which having been exported to Jersey in March 1959 for use by Jersey Motor Transport, had to be re-registered MGP11P when returned to mainland Britain in 1975. It is seen here leaving Chiswick Works on a training mission on 14/7/78. This RTL was later exported to Spain in 1982.

**Not many** RTLs survived to be preserved due to so many having been exported, but one that was is RTL1163, which appeared at the 1988 Barking Rally, of which I was one of the organisers!

**Seen dumped** at the rear of Stonebridge Park garage on 7/4/69, RTW430 and RTL684 have not only been cannibalised for spare parts for Ceylon, but also vandalised by the feral youths which already infested this area in the late 1960s. Both were taken away for scrap in May 1969.